Best Practices in Multichannel Operations & Fulfillment

By
Curt Barry

F. Curtis Barry & Company
Richmond, Virginia

Additional copies can be purchased from F. Curtis Barry & Company, 1897 Billingsgate Circle, Suite 102, Richmond, VA 23238, 804-740-8743 or contact Jeff Barry via email at jbarry@fcbco.com. You can also purchase them online by going to www.Amazon.com and searching the database.

The authors and editors who compiled this book have tried to make all the contents as accurate as possible. Authors and publisher assume no liability for damages or losses incurred in using the best practices.

ISBN 13:978-1-4196-9298-7

F. Curtis Barry & Company

Multichannel Operations & Fulfillment Consultants

Acknowledgments

First and foremost I want to thank the wonderful management of our client companies. Through our collaborative consulting assignments we have both improved their businesses and learned much from each other. I am proud to say they represent many of the leaders in multichannel marketing. I have attempted to list all these clients in the following pages; my apologies if I left any out.

Since 1985, we have written literally hundreds of articles and speeches for *Multichannel Merchant, Catalog Success, Internet Retailer, Operations & Fulfillment, Target Marketing, Fund Raising Success, Catalogue & e-Business* (UK), *Catalog Age,* Direct Marketing Association publications, conferences, newsletters, and blogs. Many editors and publishers gave me the opportunity to share what was happening in the world of multichannel operations and fulfillment. Without these opportunities, most of this material would not have been written.

For igniting my passion for multichannel marketing, I credit two people: David Waters, (then the chairman of Garfinckel's, Brooks Brothers, Miller & Rhoads, Inc. and later General Mills Retail Specialty Group) and consultant Al Schmidt. They had the vision in the mid-1970s for "remote non-store retailing" and their leadership started the first catalog at Brooks Brothers. I learned and benefited from being part of the fulfillment and systems team.

Thanks to my first client, Tiffany & Co.—Bill Chaney, Larry West and Kevin O'Halloran—for their belief in me as we developed their first catalog order management system.

I owe much to the father of fulfillment, customer service and DMA Hall of Fame honoree, the late Stanley Fenvessy, for his encouragement to expand my practice to include systems, fulfillment, customer service, benchmarking and inventory management. His ethics, hard work and quality practices were a model for me.

I thank consultant Jim Alexander for his friendship and teaching, which has given me many new and growing perspectives on strategic planning, merchandising and marketing.

Catalog circulation and marketing list brokerage founder, Don Mokrynski, taught me much about the basics of circulation planning and customer acquisition.

Over the years, the employees of F. Curtis Barry & Company have generated much of the material in the articles and in this book. Without them nothing would be possible.

To my family and my wife, Mary Sue, I appreciate their love, support in my endeavors and understanding about the long hours away from home.

I thank God and all of you for a fulfilling career and your friendship.

About F. Curtis Barry & Company

F. Curtis Barry & Company is a nationally recognized operations and fulfillment consultancy providing service to the Catalog, e-Commerce, and Retail industries. For the past 23 years, we have collaboratively developed actionable solutions for our multichannel clients that combine both proven industry best practices with the latest technology available in the industry. These solutions become part of the foundation for our clients' successes in warehouse operations, inventory management, new channel start-ups, call center operations, distribution efficiencies, etc.

Our clients like working with us because we improve their total profitability, boost their efficiencies and productivity, and lower their operating costs and expenses. We work collaboratively with our clients in the following areas of service:

- multichannel business systems;
- warehouse and distribution;
- contact center services;
- forecasting and inventory management;
- strategic, financial and operational planning;
- freight analysis; and
- Benchmarking ShareGroups and Executive Forums.

You can find out more about our multichannel operations and fulfillment consulting firm on the web at www.fcbco.com or by calling 804-740-8743. Be sure to also check out our weekly blog site at www.fcbco-blog.com for our opinions and insight on the multichannel industry.

Selected F. Curtis Barry & Company Clients

1-800 Flowers

A. M. Leonard

Abbey Press

Abercrombie & Fitch

Adirondack Direct

Ailin LLC

American Cancer Society

American Eagle Outfitters

American Express Publishing

Anthropologie

Appleseed's

Arizona Mail Order

Art Institute of Chicago

Athleta

B. A. Mason Shoes

Bare Necessities

Barrie Pace

Belk

Ben Meadows

Bensussen Deutsche

Blair Corporation

Bluefly.com

BlueSky Brands

Bra Smyth

Bradley Direct

Brooks Brothers

Brookstone

Brylane

Cabela's

Camellia & Main

Camping World

Campmor

CarDomain

Carrot-Top Industries

Catalog Ventures

Charming Shoppes

Cheap Joe's Art Stuff

Cheryl & Co.

Children's Wear Digest

Cleaner's Supply

Collections, Etc.

Colonial Williamsburg

Country Life Vitamins

Crutchfield

Cushman Fruit

Cutter & Buck

Day-Timers

Design Toscano

Design Within Reach

Dick Blick

Discovery Health

Dog.com

Doheny Enterprises

Draper's & Damon's

Dress Barn

Entertainment Earth

Esprit

Exclusively Weddings

EziBuy

Famous Smoke Shop

Fire Mountain Gems

fragranceX.com

Frederick's of Hollywood

Gander Mountain

Garden Botanika

Gardener's Supply

Garnet Hill

Garrett Wade

Getty Images

Good Guys

Gorsuch

Griot's Garage

Hanna Andersson

Hanover Direct

Harold's Stores

Harrod's

Herrington Catalog

Highlights For Children

Home Care Delivered

Home Trends

Hubbard Peanuts

illy caffe

International AutoSport

International Spy Museum

Intuit

J & P Cycles

J. Baker

J. Jill

J. Peterman

JC Whitney

Jewelry Television by ACN

JoS. A. Bank

Junonia

Kable Products Services

Kiehl's

L. L. Bean

Lands' End

LifeWay Christian Resources

Lighthouse International

Lillian Vernon

Littleton Coin Company

Magellan's

Maritz Rewards

Mary Maxim

Maus & Hoffman

Memphis Net & Twine

MindWare

Missionary Oblates

Monterey Bay Clothing

Motherwear

Mrs. Field's Cookies

Mustang Group

N.E.E.D.S.

National Geographic Society

National Wildlife Federation

Neiman Marcus Direct

Nordstrom

Norm Thompson Outfitters	Shop At Home Network	The Vermont Country Store
Northern Safety	Sierra Trading Post	The Wet Seal
Overton's	Smith & Hawken	THT Designs
Park Seed	Southwest Indian Foundation	Tiffany & Co.
Pendleton Woolen Mills	Specialty Catalog	Touch of Class
Peruvian Connection	Sports Endeavors	Touchstone
Petals	Starbucks Coffee Company	Travel Oregon
PetEdge	Steele Rubber	Travers Tools Co.
Plow & Hearth	Storehouse Furniture	Uniform Advantage
Positive Promotions	Stumps	Urban Outfitters
Power Systems	Sur La Table	Venus Swimwear
Publishers Clearing House	Sure Fit Slipcovers	Vermont Teddy Bear Co.
Restoration Hardware	Talbot's	Virginia Diner
Revival Animal Health	The Baker's Catalogue	Walter Drake
Rocky Mountain ATV	The Metropolitan Museum of Art	West Marine
Ross-Simons	The Orvis Company	Westport
S & S Worldwide	The Potpourri Group	What On Earth
Saks Folio	The Service Center	Wind & Weather
Sales Service America	The Smithsonian Catalogue	WinterSilks
SeaBear	The Swiss Colony	Winterthur
Shades of Light	The Thompson Group	Zaner Bloser

Selected Client Testimonials

"As we were in the midst of implementing a new order management system we wanted to be sure that our plan was comprehensive, utilized best practices and had realistic timeframes to mitigate the risk. We engaged F. Curtis Barry & Company to review our plan, assist in user testing and project management oversight, and render an opinion at critical points whether the project was on task to be delivered as planned. With the guidance and recommendations of F. Curtis Barry & Company we were able to focus on critical items and successfully implement our new system.

We then engaged F. Curtis Barry & Company to perform a search and selection for a new e-commerce solution for us. F. Curtis Barry & Company were diligent and thorough in meeting with the staff here to understand the business needs we had and translate those needs into requirements that were used to search for viable e-commerce vendors. Their knowledge of the vendors and systems allowed us to focus on our core business. F. Curtis Barry and Company did a superb job in analyzing and developing the requirements, and recommending e-commerce solutions that fit our specific business needs."

Kathy Lijoi
Director of Information Technology Services
The Vermont Country Store

"Just about anyone in the catalog/multichannel business seeking out expert advice on any and all fulfillment issues turns to Curt Barry and his firm. You ask Curt a question, you know you're not only getting years of experience in his heavily-loaded response, but what's more, his solutions take into account all the latest advances in operations and fulfillment."

Paul Miller
Editor in Chief
Catalog Success magazine

"A long-time contributor to Multichannel Merchant magazine, Curt Barry is one of the industry leaders on operations and fulfillment for multiple selling channels."

Melissa Dowling
Editor-in-Chief
Multichannel Merchant magazine

"It may be a cliché, but it's true: What the folks at F. Curtis Barry & Company don't know about multichannel operations isn't worth knowing. Just as important, they can communicate that knowledge so that even novices can be in the know as well."

Sherry Chiger
Editorial Director
Catalogue | e-business

"How do you start to replace a 17-year-old operating system when you are not familiar with the latest technology or the track records and reputations of the myriad of potential vendors selling operating systems in today's marketplace?

The answer was relatively simple for our organization. We were fortunate to have a guide who provided us with an honest and sincere evaluation of the operating software that best fit our needs after their detailed analysis. For NEEDS, Inc., that guide was F. Curtis Barry & Company (FCBCO).

The consultants from FCBCO did not try to shoehorn a "canned" operating software system into our company. Instead, they talked to our employees and constructed a script which we used as a roadmap over a nine-day interview process with three software finalists. Each finalist made a detailed presentation and demonstration of their operating system to our entire Management Team based on the script provided by FCBCO. This process uncovered the pluses and minuses associated with each system.

The involvement of FCBCO personnel continued right through our Team's follow-up evaluations after each of the demonstrations. As we discussed the potential trade-offs of one operating system versus another, FCBCO helped us clearly prioritize our true objectives of this system conversion.

Now, nearly eighteen months after our implementation, it is clear to our company that we were led through this process with great effectiveness and efficiency by FCBCO personnel which has made this operating system conversion a truly successful venture for NEEDS, Inc., its employees, and its customers."

Andrew S. Fox
President/CEO
NEEDS, Inc.

"Over the past 8 years we have relied on F. Curtis Barry & Company for a number of projects including the layout design and systems review for our in-house B to B distribution center, 3PL searches and placement related to our B to C Catalog business as well as operating reviews for our internal and external DC's and Contact Center. With each of these projects F. Curtis Barry & Company has been able to supplement our in-house staff with industry expertise and contacts that we could never feasibly develop in-house. We have found that the team at F. Curtis Barry & Company is particularly good at tailoring a consulting engagement to meet our specific needs whether it is a one day or multi-week project."

Richard Eaton
Vice President, Operations
Highlights for Children Inc.

"F. Curtis Barry & Company has been a great consulting resource for several reasons:

- They have deep knowledge of the multi channel model and its inherent challenges and complexity.
- Because of their deep knowledge we do not have to spend time and money educating them on the typical project which translates to less time spent and a lower cost than might otherwise be incurred
- They can be relied on to stay within scope and budget of the project as agreed to"

John Rice
Vice President of Finance and Operations
PetEdge

"Travel Oregon hired F. Curtis Barry & Company to assist in the search, selection, and contract negotiation of a third party fulfillment vendor. Today there are a variety of vendors in the market place who offer a broad spectrum of services and having F. Curtis Barry & Company there to provide sound analysis and recommendations based on their experience assured we had the information needed to make the right decisions for our business."

Kevin Wright
Director, Consumer Marketing
Travel Oregon

"I've relied on the expertise of F. Curtis Barry & Company for many years. I have done several projects with this team and have always been pleased with their quality of work, their integrity and their ability to provide timely information and solutions. I have never hesitated to pick up the phone to ask questions about logistics, benchmarks or warehousing because I trust their knowledge and value their opinion."

Marie Lapetina
Operations Manager, Products
Colonial Williamsburg Foundation

"We have worked with F. Curtis Barry & Company on a wide range of projects including search for operating systems, call center and DC operations. With each project we have found that this group has brought a tremendous depth of knowledge and experience to the project. Before jumping into recommendations they work to understand the business and culture. Each project we have implemented with the help of F. Curtis Barry & Company has provided outstanding results."

Randy Rieder
Vice President Operations
Hanna Andersson

Best Practices in Multichannel Operations & Fulfillment

By
Curt Barry

F. Curtis Barry & Company
Richmond, Virginia

Table of Contents

Contact Center

Forecasting & Inventory Management

Direct Commerce Systems

Warehouse & Distribution

Introduction

Just for a minute, let's take a look at the fulfillment process. Fulfillment includes all the processes involved in taking, filling, and servicing customer orders from e-commerce, catalog, space ads, requests, kiosks and other direct order sources.

Four major components are basic to the fulfillment process:

- Contact Center
- Warehouse or Fulfillment Center
- Inventory
- Systems

The **Contact Center** is the first line of customer service, whether dealing with customers over the phone, supporting them on the web site or dealing with customer complaints and inquires. Companies must address attrition, team building and training, reducing the cost of taking orders, outsourcing, etc. key issues as they work to move the business from a high percentage of phone orders to the majority being e-commerce.

To be efficient, the **Fulfillment Center** requires effective management of the processes of receiving and storing product and filling customer orders. Those processes include the movement of product through receiving, checking, quality assurance, stock put away, replenishment of pick faces, picking, packing, shipping and manifesting, returns processing as well as inventory control. Storing more product and shipping more customer orders with the same resources is the mantra of many companies. Outbound transportation costs have accelerated to the point where they exceed direct labor expense. Equally important to an efficient fulfillment process is the effective use of the physical assets—including the layout and material handling equipment—of the center.

Then there is the largest balance sheet asset in most multichannel businesses: the **Inventory**. For a product seller, being without the right inventory means there cannot be a high level of customer service or profitability. But without planning the optimal levels of inventory—the delicate balance between too much and too little of the right products—there can be no profitability. Other areas for process improvement include the accuracy of the merchandise planning process and of weekly forecasting, cost of inbound freight, the high cost of back orders to customer service and profitability and supply chain efficiency.

This brings us to our fourth component: **Systems**. For decades, direct and multichannel marketing have relied on systems to streamline the business process, provide online customer service, move products through the fulfillment center and provide the marketing information to acquire customers and grow the business, as well as to provide planning, forecasting and analysis systems for the merchant.

However, as businesses become more complex, selecting and implementing the right customer service, warehouse management, marketing and merchandising systems takes considerably more financial investment and time. And there isn't any such thing as the "perfect system"; as a company grows and evolves so do its IT needs and the need for adaptation of the most cost effective technology.

There are truly multichannel enterprise-wide systems starting to be adopted, although they have a long way to go to be considered comprehensive. Emphasis in many companies is on replacing aging order management and warehouse management systems that have been in place for 10-15 years, with technology that is more user friendly, cost effective and integrated.

This book is divided into sections on management, contact center, inventory, systems and warehouse to better assist you. Throughout all of these component processes, there is one common element upon which success depends: our *People*. How successful a business is rests on how well we motivate and manage people to take care of the customer. Many of these articles focus on the people aspects involved in the processes.

Our motivation for this book—a monograph of articles on best practices in fulfillment—is to create a resource which helps the multichannel executive to better plan and manage the people, balance sheet assets and inventory involved in the total fulfillment process. The goal is to provide a high level of customer service at a fair profit that will allow the business to sustain itself.

In working as a consultant in many of America's most successful and profitable multichannel businesses, we have learned that a company's size doesn't determine its level of adoption of best practices, its efficiency, whether it has effective systems or its profitability. Many smaller companies can excel where larger companies need improvement. We hope this book assists you in implementing best practices throughout your organization.

This book addresses practices that will make your operation more efficient and allow you to serve the customer in a more timely fashion. Like the "perfect system"—which is never completed—the book is a work in progress, which we look forward to expanding in later editions. There are many other articles and opinions on our website at www.fcbco.com and on our blog at www.fcbco-blog.com.

Business Management

70+ Ways to Reduce Costs, Increase Productivity and Improve Customer Service

By Curt Barry

Over the past 23 years F. Curtis Barry & Company's work with multichannel companies in operations and fulfillment consulting has allowed us to compile these 70+ ways that can cut costs and increase productivity, which will ultimately lead to an improvement in customer service. We have focused our cost reduction and productivity assessment efforts in the following four major areas:

Contact Center

Scheduling and staffing models, service levels and technology in the call center are all affected by the increasing eCommerce order volumes. What are the ways to be more efficient and serve the customer better from the contact center?

Warehouse & Distribution

With most companies coming out of a less than perfect holiday season, there is a real need to increase productivity without having to make major capital purchases to do so. Discover ways to reduce your warehouse cost per order, increase capacity without expansion and improve service levels.

Forecasting & Inventory Management

Inventory is most companies' largest balance sheet asset. How it's managed determines customer service and profitability. Learn ways to improve the management of this asset.

Multichannel Business Systems

Order management, warehouse, e-commerce and inventory management systems are at the heart of the company. These systems affect the productivity and sales of all departments including merchandising, marketing, fulfillment and contact center. Investigate ways to plan for, select and implement effective Multichannel Business Systems.

We ask that you please consider using F. Curtis Barry & Company's consulting services to tailor a cost reduction and productivity improvement assessment to your company's needs in order to evaluate, develop and implement these improvements and cost reduction practices.

25 ways to be more efficient and serve the customer better in the contact center

F. Curtis Barry & Company has successfully assisted our client's contact centers by increasing productivity of personnel; applying technology for scheduling, email management, IVR and training; improving customer service for serving online customers; and selecting and installing order management systems. Some of our multichannel contact center clients include Appleseed's, The Metropolitan Museum of Art, Day-Timers, Blair, Hanna Andersson, Haband, and Norm Thompson.

Perform post season audit
Determine what went really well, what needed a band aid to get ac-

complished and what were severe problems. Operational assessment of metrics, productivity, service levels, attrition, revenue generation and process improvements which should be considered.

Benchmarking

Set up internal benchmarks to reduce your cost per order, cost per call, cost per contact and cost per transaction. Translate these down to department and individual work standards.

Join F. Curtis Barry & Company's Contact Center Benchmarking ShareGroup to exchange metrics and best practices, discuss strategies, network with peers, and tour and audit a member's contact center.

Staffing models - full time/part time/flex

Labor is your single biggest expense in the contact center. Take a good look at your current staffing ratio. Full time, if not kept productive, may be costly. Change the mix of full time, part time and flex time staff.

Attrition (turnover)

Studies show that attrition costs $3,000 to $10,000 in recruiting, training and initial on the job investment to bring a new person on board. Many contact centers average 40% to 50% or higher. Review the reasons why attrition is so high and put a plan together to reduce it.

Outsourcing

Domestic, off shore or near shore for phone, email, mail orders and other documents, etc. So many choices for so many options, you really need to have assistance—but you can save money! Investigate and implement it without sacrificing your quality, customer service or your revenue.

Training

Review your training plans and make sure the agents are trained in training sessions, not On the Job Training! This will create shorter "ramp up" times for new hires. A solid, well thought out training plan will pay great dividends and improve customer service. Keep it all consistent to keep the knowledge levels high.

Measure by interval and not the day
This will create a need to stay focused and find efficiencies in scheduling and processes. You cannot make it up later in the day; if you missed one interval you lost money, either with labor or sales.

Use QA to drive out unneeded processes
If you are not, then you should conduct a review of your processes from a Quality Review point of view. Make sure your Quality Team has three MAIN constituencies in mind as they do their jobs...#1, first and foremost, the paying customer; #2, the company; and #3, the supervisors and the agents for training and coaching. Now make sure that there are not other items the agents do that don't support these efforts.

Adherence
If you are suffering during scheduling intervals, make sure your personnel are in the seats at the right time.

Occupancy
Manage this gingerly. If done correctly you will run a well oiled machine. If you miss, you will hemorrhage money. Scheduling is the key to maintaining optimal occupancy rates.

Workforce software
Many companies are still using Excel for their staffing software. Excel cannot save you as much money year over year as a good workforce program. Team up with Fulfillment Center to share the system. It will pay for itself quickly. If you have one, understand how to use it

to its maximum.

Service level review

Are you at the right service level for your customers' needs? Or are you following a standard that is too high? If so, you are spending a great deal of extra money which may not be necessary.

Supervisors

Review your supervisor-to-agent ratio. Are you overstaffed with supervisors or understaffed with supervisors?

Speech recognition (VRU)

To some, Speech Recognition is an evil word. But many companies have used it selectively to save a great deal of money. You can, if engineered correctly and your expectations are realistic.

Interactive voice response

Are you using it to the best advantage? Contact centers use IVR systems to identify and segment callers (orders versus customer service). This allows the center to tailor services according to the customer request.

Telecomm audit

Make sure you are not paying for services, numbers or locations that you don't have any longer. You could be spending a great deal more than you need. It is estimated that over 50% of all corporate telephone bills have errors.

Call flow review / prompts

Too many branches or prompts will confuse and irritate the customer and cost you telecom charges. Keep it simple; the customer will love you and you can get call types other ways for reporting.

Home agents

Add flexibility to your staffing model and reduce the center's occupancy costs. Understand what the legal ramifications, supervision, home office work environment and technology aspects are. You can save money and have happy employees.

Shared labor

Need help with peak labor? Some companies have found a partner that is contra-seasonal within or outside your niche. This allows you to manage the peaks, reduce start up training expenses and you may be able to barter for time (minutes used).

Using an agency for peaks

If you just can't staff for the peak, seek out a good temporary agency. Contact centers make good use of them, managing like you would your own staff.

Email management software

Get onboard with an ASP and start saving on your labor with email and chat functions. It is a win for the customer and a win for you.

Cross selling/up-selling

Remember your agents are the eyes and ears to your customers in most cases, so make them your best sales force. More companies need to look at this as a way to increase average order. Will you use incentives to achieve higher results? Your agents can do it effectively and not be offensive to the customer.

Analyze call reasons, drive out unneeded call drivers

Understand why the customers are calling. You might have found an area that needs to be reengineered.

Chat with the customer to secure the sale / drive down calls

If you can engage the customer on the website you should be able to sell them or close the sale for them with chat. Don't let the shopping cart go empty.

Use KPI's to meet your goals and keep an eye on expenses
If you focus on the right things you will know where your money is going every day, week or month. Measure what is important and keep an eye on it.

20 ways to reduce your cost per order, increase capacity without expansion and improve service levels in warehouse and fulfillment

F. Curtis Barry & Company's assessments are tailor-made to identify your needs and potential improvements to process, layout and use of space, staff productivity, systems and freight analysis. We have been successful in lowering the cost per order, increasing storage capacity within the center, reducing inbound and outbound freight, improving service levels and turnaround times. Fulfillment clients include Positive Promotions, Publishers Clearing House, Sea Bear, Hanna Andersson, LifeWay Christian Resources, Cabela's, Abercrombie & Fitch, The Metropolitan Museum of Art, Belk Inc., Sur La Table, Crutchfield, Urban Outfitters, and Colonial Williamsburg Foundation; to name just a few.

Benchmarking
A program to set up internal benchmarks will reduce your cost per order or hold the cost in line as volumes increase. Translate these down to department and individual work standards.

Join F. Curtis Barry & Company's Warehouse Benchmarking Share-Group to exchange metrics and best practices, network with peers, discuss fulfillment strategies, and tour and audit a member's warehouse.

Manage the labor force

Labor is the largest controllable expense item in your DC. Successful practices to improve performance can lower your labor cost.

Hiring, retention and attrition (turnover)

Labor is your first or second largest expense after outbound freight in the fulfillment center. Review the reasons attrition is so high and work to close the gap. Review your hiring, retention and training practices. How well are you able to staff for the peaks?

Reduce handling and touches

The fewer touches of product, the less cost of shipping an order. Streamline the operation and apply industry best practices to reduce handling and cost of fulfilling an order.

Slotting

Effective slotting practices can lower your costs for picking, replenishment, and putaway warehouse labor.

Team building

Successful organizations take team building seriously. Take your organization to a new level and improve productivity.

Picking options

How can you use best practices to improve picking productivity?

Use what you have more productively

This is a mantra in fulfillment today. Our assessments will help you get more productivity from your layout, space/product storage utilization and staff. By not caring for the basics of fulfillment, you are adding costs to the warehouse operation. Increasing current capacity and utilizing that capacity more effectively are key objectives. We believe in getting as much productivity as possible out of the existing layout, processes and systems first.

Performance reporting
The old adage of, "You can't improve what you don't measure" is certainly true. An effective measurement and reporting process can improve performance and lower costs.

Packing options
How can industry best practices help you improve performance and reduce costs of one of the most labor intensive functions in the warehouse?

Freight management
Controlling inbound and outbound freight can make the difference between a profit or loss for your business.

Use proper levels of qa
Are you "over inspecting" activities to the point of diminishing returns and spending money that does not result in a return on the investment?

Receiving practices and cross docking
Cross docking is an effective practice to reduce handling and costs while improving customer service and shipping costs.

Process returns more efficiently
Returns cost more than orders to process. Untimely processing of customer credits, refunds and exchanges can damage customer service. Our assessments look at use of staff, people, space and systems to improve productivity.

Workforce software
Many companies are still using Excel for their staffing software. Ex-

cel cannot save you as much money year over year as a good work-force program. Team up with Contact Center to share a scheduling system. It will pay for itself quickly. If you have one, understand how to use it to its maximum.

Outsourcing option

There are practical and cost effective reasons to outsource part or all of your business. It may be to deal with a peak, new product categories or when fulfillment is not a company core competency.

Finding the right level of automation and systems

ROI analysis could put automation into your planning for cost improvement. The wrong material handling equipment can be creating hidden lost time and inefficient product flow, impacting cost and customer service.

Warehouse management/bar code systems

This should include reviewing how bar coding throughout the warehouse, conveyance, material handling and warehouse management systems can improve productivity, increase service levels and reduce costs.

Inventory management in the warehouse

Effective inventory management is the single most important tool to improve customer service and reduce cost of operation.

Replenishment practices

Effective replenishment is the basis of successful order fulfillment. Inefficient replenishment will cost huge dollars and negatively impact customer service.

17 ways to improve management of forecasting and inventory

F. Curtis Barry & Companies has worked with many multichannel companies to: improve the management of the inventory assets; enhance planning, forecasting and analysis; modify organizational structure to be more efficient; and to implement more effective forecasting and

inventory management systems. Some of our clients include Chadwick's, Brylane, Charming Shoppes, The Art Institute of Chicago, Gardener's Supply, PetEdge, Bare Necessities, Frederick's of Hollywood, Highlights For Children, LifeWay Christian Resources.

Benchmarking
Have you developed the necessary metrics for initial customer order fill rates, final fill, inventory turnover, gross margin, lost margin from liquidation, age of inventory, etc.? In turn have these become performance objectives for the Inventory Control Buyers?

From an external benchmarking basis, join the F. Curtis Barry & Company's Forecasting & Inventory Management Benchmarking ShareGroup. Exchange metrics on a blind basis, learn best practices on process, systems, organization, etc., as well as network with your peers.

Streamline process
Assess the processes of seasonal planning, weekly forecasting, end-of-season analysis for your multichannel business. Streamline how the Inventory Control buyers perform their work and manage inventory. Process improvement should improve planning and forecasting accuracy, and lead to improvement in customer initial order fill rate and turnover.
Know your vendors
What are their pain points (space, cash, capacity)? What are their

strengths? Understand these thoroughly to gain maximum leverage. Should you reduce the number of vendors you purchase from to get more leverage?

Establish a vendor scorecard
Involve Merchandising, Inventory Control, Fulfillment and Accounting and set up a vendor scorecard to evaluate vendors. This should include sales, margin, on-time delivery, significant problems, etc. Review it several times a year with the vendors. You may even want to take it a step further and set up a vendor recognition program for the top vendors.

Visit your top 20 vendors now
Strengthens relationships. Include at least the Merchant and Inventory Control Buyer. Involve vendor's senior management as well as yours. Have an agenda about your company's direction, needs and expectations.

Manage your vendors
Insist on costs, terms, and conditions with vendors that make sense for your company. It is your responsibility to look out for your interests, theirs to look out for theirs! Develop vendor compliance and charge back policies to enforce compliance.

Negotiate terms
Arrange and pay 2%10Net60 with all domestic vendors.

Provide limitless access to information systems
Inventory Control Buyers must have laptops and VPN access to all tools. Pays for itself quickly and frequently.

Invest in systems
Provide Inventory Control Buyers easy, efficient, accurate, and timely

access to data. Ongoing training, report requests, modification requests should be a management priority. This group spends more money than any other. Support them!

Invest in inventory control staff
The Inventory Control Department manages the largest balance sheet asset in the company. Hire and retain strong people, provide them tools, have high expectations of them, then reward their solid performance well. Should you have a different organizational structure?

Consistent forecasting philosophy
Be sure all categories and SKUs are forecast using consistent methodology that fits your organization. Challenge it often.

Review, recite, retain key data
IC Buyers MUST know their category and vendor inventory levels, turns, SKU count, and GM $ and %. More importantly, understand the impact of their actions to these metrics and to the business.

Clear a day's-work-in-a-day
Ensure timely and accurate data across the organization by demanding all receipts, put away, invoices, PO acknowledgments, orders, (all business transactions) are posted daily.

Renegotiate (always)
New PO's for in-season replenishment of items selling over forecast are due better costs. Ask early and assertively for RTV and/or mark down money for poor performers.

Liquidation
Is your company aggressive enough in identifying potential overstocks and putting them into one of 15 different methods used in multichannel companies? Reduce slow selling stock as close to in-season

as possible to gain a higher cost recovery.

<u>Inbound freight</u>
Have a qualified consultant perform a freight audit to see what additional savings can be gained. Join a freight consortium to maximize savings.

<u>Importing</u>
Imported products now represent 50% to 70% of all products in many companies and they give a considerably higher initial mark up and maintained margin. Is your staff managing this inventory effectively? They require longer lead times and higher vendor minimums, which can lead to higher inventories and slower turnover.

11 ways to plan for, select and implement effective multichannel business systems

F. Curtis Barry & Company has improved the effectiveness of multichannel businesses by assisting companies in defining user requirements, final system selection and project management of the installation of the multichannel business systems. Clients include The Metropolitan Museum of Art, West Marine, Cabela's, Cheap Joe's Art Stuff, Revival Animal Health, Campmor, Abercrombie & Fitch, Anthropologie, The Vermont Country Store, Sport Endeavors, 1-800 Flowers, Tiffany & Co. and Neiman Marcus Direct.

<u>Project planning</u>
Proper project planning and the appropriate staffing to support large complex implementation is one of the most critical aspects to reducing unnecessary risks, delivering the application on time and within the budget. A qualified consultant can either project manage or assist your staff in this critical activity.

Post implementation audit

At conversion, companies typically use 25% to 35% of a new system's function effectively. Audit the implementation 30 to 60 days
after conversion to evaluate what the software vendor still has not delivered; audit your staff's responsibilities; itemize how additional
training can improve system use; what additional functionality should
be scheduled for implementation, what data conversion problems still
exist, etc.

Return on investment

Understanding how applications will achieve an acceptable ROI will
assist with the justification of new applications. Measure the expected
or planned ROI against the actual ROI for both savings and intangible
(soft) benefits.

Enhanced management reporting

By developing more targeted reports of key metrics and benchmarks,
management will be able to stay in touch with what's happening
across the enterprise. Develop key performance indicators (KPIs),
corporate dashboards and effective reporting for each function or department.

Enhanced systems integration

By developing more detailed integrations, manual processes and lack
of data between systems can be eliminated, thus reducing errors and
bottlenecks and decreasing expenses. Enhanced systems integration
will also decrease the need for redundant data between applications.

Get more from your computer application

There is always personnel turnover, or companies lose key users of
applications. Identify departments and individuals that can benefit

from additional training. This will allow you to set up educational programs to address their needs and the company gets improved productivity and analysis.

Single source of data

This goes hand in hand with enhanced systems integrations. By reducing the number of times data has to be replicated in various systems, companies can reduce overhead and the potential for errors in redundant data.

Contract programmers

Where applicable, this can help reduce the costs of critical enhancements to applications. It can be difficult to find qualified people to hire, in which case, contracting with IT/programming professionals can be more cost effective then attempting to hire programmers.

Software As A Service (SAAS)

SAAS models can allow companies to reduce the initial investment necessary to implement and maintain applications. By not having to invest in hardware or staffing to maintain an application, companies can reduce their IT expenses. Typical SAAS models place the responsibility of hardware and software maintenance and upgrades with the vendor, reducing staff and expenses. A company only owns usage rights while contracted and does not own licensing rights to the product.

Outsourcing

Multichannel businesses have the option to outsource the hardware with various companies in order to reduce staffing and maintenance related expenses. Companies can choose to outsource their existing hardware or shift their applications to new hardware at the outsourcing facility.

<u>Use of consultants for development</u>

Using outside consultants and programmers for application development can reduce long term expenses. In addition, outsourcing programming and application development can reduce the need for recruitment and retention of qualified programmers.

What Are Your Shipping Options?

By Curt Barry

In the next few weeks, all the carriers will complete their 2008 pricing announcements. As we look at the future, it's probably a good bet that these carriers' rates aren't going down any more than the cost of oil. So what's the impact and action plan for your business? Given the size of the increases that have been announced so far, multichannel companies need to look at all the options open to them and develop short and long-term strategies to reduce the impact.

UPS has announced that they will be increasing Ground rates by 4.9% in 2008, which is equal to last year. (FedEx will most likely match the UPS Ground increase, but that information has not yet been released.) Under new rates, the Ground commercial zone 2, 1-lb. rate has increased 5.0% over last year—overall, a 16% increase over three years, from $3.62 in 2005 to $4.20 in 2008. For 1-70 lb. packages the average increase is 4.8%. However, if the majority of your shipments are in zones 4 or 5 –like many businesses are- the increase is about 5.16%. Depending on your warehouse location and the predominant zones in which you ship to customers, the impact could be more or less than this average. Meanwhile, the Ground residential minimum charge increased to $6.15, a combination of the base rate for zone 2 and the Ground residential surcharge. In a quick survey of shipping tables of 66 multichannel companies, we found that 71% of the tables were lower than this $6.15 minimum charge.

As AFMS Logistics Management Group's Managing Director Rick Collins points out, "The announced rate increases of 4.9% for Ground and 6.9% for Air from FedEx and UPS masks the true impact for many shippers. The base rates may average the announced increases across the board; however higher zone express shippers could experience increases in the 9-10% range. Additionally, surcharges are increasing up to 20% in some cases. Surcharges for irregular and large packages are up 8.3% to 12.5%. Commercial remote add-ons are increasing 7.1% and residential fees are up 5.4% for Ground."

All is not totally gloom. There was some good news on November 15, when the Postal Service Governors announced that future prices will be adjusted using new regulations issued by the Postal Regulatory Commission (PRC) on October 29. Consistent with the Postal Accountability and Enhancement Act of 2006, future price increases for mailing services will be capped at the rate of inflation. Said Postmaster General John E Potter, "This delivers one of the main goals of the new law for business mailers—a predictable price schedule." The new pricing regulations give the Postal Service added flexibility for shipping services. "We intend to use this new flexibility to grow our competitive business," said Potter, "offering volume discounts and contract pricing."

Looking at the industry as a whole, however, Edward Wolfe, transportation stock analyst for Bear Stearns & Co., had this to say: "Our sense is FedEx is clearly trying to send a message of pricing strength to both its customers and to competitors UPS and DHL."

I think we've gotten the message. Now we need to do everything we can to reduce costs.

With the continual increases in the cost of oil and shipping, we think that companies need to assess both short and longer-term strategies.

Here are 15 short- and long-term options to investigate:

1. Renegotiate your contract.

2. Can you use USPS to your advantage?

3. Are you using best-way rate shopping?

4. Consider package weighing, and take out inserts when they push the package into a higher bracket.

5. Can you leverage economies of scale using the same carriers for inbound and outbound freight?

6. Investigate the economics of a second warehouse to reduce the distance and cost to ship to the customer.

7. Reassess your shipping and handling table in light of the changes.

8. If you're going to use free shipping, re-assess the minimum dollar order value and its effects on your transportation costs. Should the minimum be increased?

9. Review whether you should use by-item shipping charges in your web and catalog copy for heavy and oversize products.

10. Can you make use of package consolidators and zone skipping?

11. Assess your total operation and determine if other costs can be reduced to help offset these increases.

12. Improve your inventory forecasting and systems to improve in-

ventory position and decrease the cost of back orders; keep in mind the $6.15 Ground residential minimum charge.

13. From marketing and merchandising perspectives, how can the average order value be increased so that shipping cost is not such a large percent of the average or small order?

14. Review your policies for giving away free freight to return merchandise.

15. Is it time to use an experienced transportation consulting company to help you get savings? Or are you big enough to hire an internal specialist to continually assess and hopefully lower your costs?

Contract renegotiation is your #1 weapon. How much can be saved will depend on a number of factors: how well prepared you are in terms of knowing your package shipping profile; knowledge of carrier pricing and what can be discounted and negotiated; the 70+ accessorial charges and how they make up your total costs, etc. An increase in the carrier's list rates does not necessarily translate to higher shipping costs. Bear Stearns' Wolfe says, "At this point, we continue to expect the market, not announced large rate increases, to determine the direction of pricing." "The market" means competitive bidding and your ability to negotiate. Another factor to consider is how important your account is to the depot or hub. We've learned that sometimes smaller accounts are much more important than management might realize, given the outbound volume.

The most nimble multichannel companies will determine how to offset these foreboding continual increases. We believe it will take all the weapons—both short-term tactics and longer-term strategies—to keep profitability from eroding.

Employee Turnover...
What Does It Really Cost You?

By Curt Barry

Many companies see turnover as a necessary cost of doing business, especially in managing a call center or a fulfillment center. However, have you taken a good look recently at your staff turnover levels and the actual dollars this costs your company? Whether it is in fulfillment or in the contact center, the costs are high. Industry turnover averages are hovering around 40%-50%. In many call centers it may unfortunately be as high as 90%-100%. Industry experience is that turnover costs range from $3,000 to $10,000 in people time, training, testing and the ramp-up to full production. This does not include expenses for agencies, ads, etc. which must be added on.

As you research your turnover rate, here are some points to take into consideration.

Statistics you'll want to collect:

- Number of employees hired
- Number of employees who started training
- Number of employees who leave while in training
- The number who leave once they graduate to the production staff

Analyses you'll want to undertake:

- The amount of time and associated costs for the human resources department, supervisors and managers to recruit and interview
- Reasons for leaving (collected during exit interviews)
- Length of the training class (training overload or under-training?)
- Size of the training class (amount of personal attention)
- Schedule availability of the trainer to conduct the classes
- Costs for testing, background checks, drug testing and skills testing
- Mentoring/coaching time and cost for the agent and the coach
- Length of time and cost to get up to speed and be part of the production staff

Develop a Turnover Report

Using the contact center as an example, you need to have a defined beginning point from which to measure turnover. Let's say you start analysis April 1st (new quarter, start of the month) and your headcount is 100. You hire 10 in the month of April and you lose 17 employees. Your turnover rate is 15.5% and you have a net headcount of 93.

$100 + 10 - 17 = 93$ ..... 17 divided by $110 = 15.45\%$

In May you started with 93, added 25 new employees and lost 30 employees. Your monthly turnover is 25.4% and your year-to-date turnover is 34.8%.

$93 + 25 - 30 = 88$ ..... 30 divided by $118 = 25.42\%$; year-to-date total 47 (employees that left) divided by 135 (starting count + new hires) = 34.8%

In June, you start with 88 employees. You add 40 new hires and you lose 47 employees; your ending headcount is 81. Your turnover rate is 53.7% for the quarter.

88 + 40 – 47 = 81 .... 47 divided by 128 = 36.72%

Cumulative total for the quarter is 94 divided by 175 = 53.7%

To sum it up, your report might show the numbers as follows. Add the appropriate cost columns depending on your research above.

| | | | | | | | Cumulative Quarterly/YTD | | |
Period	Starting Count	New Hires	Total after new hires	Employees Lost	Net	Turnover %	Total after new hires	Total Lost	Turnover %
April	100	10	110	17	93	15.45	110	17	15.45
May	93	25	118	30	88	25.42	135	47	34.81
June	88	40	128	47	81	36.72	175	94	53.71

I think when we walk through these calculations it illustrates the magnitude of the amount of staff churn.

If that was not scary enough, now multiply the lost employees times the $3,000 to $10,000 we mentioned earlier (or whatever it costs your company).

94 lost employees times $3,000 = $282,000
94 lost employees times $10,000 = $940,000

As companies seek to understand turnover, many companies that use seasonal labor subtract those that were hired for the season and were terminated at season-end from their effective turnover rate. The turnover rate should be calculated both in total and after seasonal labor is subtracted.

There is another, and maybe more important, aspect to turnover – the effect on customer service and customer confidence. New employees don't know the products as well. They aren't as sure of the company's policies. They may get flustered when confronted with an irate customer. You are less apt to trust new employees or empower them to the degree you do seasoned veterans. Look at the cost of quality vs. the cost of failure to meet your customer's expectations. The cost of correcting an error is between $35 and $50 in any company. And worst of all, a dissatisfied customer may shop another multichannel company. In my mind the high service marketers in our industry are L.L. Bean, Lands' End, Cabela's, and Coldwater Creek – great models for many of us.

A path to proceed on is:

1. Set up a system to track and calculate employee turnover monthly.
2. Spend the time to research and answer the issues that are raised about turnover.
3. Establish an exit interview process to learn more about why people leave.
4. Look at the turnover by months and years of service. Are you seeing turnover with long term employees? New hires?
5. Calculate the cost of recruiting, training and losing an employee and get management to understand the reasons and the costs.
6. Set up a spreadsheet that will let you enter the monthly data and calculate the turnover and the cost to the company.
7. From there establish a plan of action for change.

Summary

Turnover is expensive, not only in operations costs but more importantly, in how we serve the customer. Your turnover may be contributing to lower sales generation.

Teamwork For World-Class Results

By Curt Barry

Q: We would like to achieve world-class results in our operation, but our efforts seem consistently to fall short of our expectations. Can you suggest ways that, as a manager, I could improve the level of teamwork in our operation?

A: The solution could be as simple as improving the level of managerial effectiveness. If you review the following eleven questions as honestly as possible, you may discover that you have only tapped the surface of your capability to achieve world-class results.

Question 1 - Do you truly understand your relationship with your staff?

Does your team perceive you as a dynamic decision-maker and planner who takes personal interest in their success? If your response is less than an emphatic yes, it is time to take a personal inventory of how you interact with your team. Begin by asking them to evaluate you, using a standard form. If the responses you receive are all complimentary and offer no constructive criticism, your staff may not be comfortable enough to be open and honest, and you have an indicator that you need to understand your relationship with each team member better.

Question 2 - What motivates staff members to excel beyond normal expected performance?

To roll individual successes into a strong team performance, a manager has to understand how to motivate individuals. When you develop goals and key performance indicators for each team member, how much time do you spend identifying how to assist each person to achieve and to exceed those goals? You can begin by considering that nearly everyone is motivated by pride and recognition. You will identify other motivating factors as you proceed.

Question 3 - Have you empowered your staff to achieve success?

Managers are responsible to develop people, and people do not develop unless given responsibility and the opportunity to fail. Allow team members to manage to their ability and assist them to develop that ability. Managers are equally responsible to constructively identify and review mistakes, indicating the impact on the organization, as a developmental tool. No one wants to be micromanaged. Give team members the opportunity to be successful on their own. It is a strong part of appealing to their pride and respect.

Question 4 - Are you reluctant to delegate tasks and responsibilities to your staff?

Unless you develop this ability you cannot successfully empower your team. You will never achieve the greatest potential level of results by thinking you can do everything better than anyone else or by wanting to make every decision.

Question 5 - Do you trust your associates to complete tasks effectively and accurately?

If you are continually checking team members' work, you need to identify quickly whether the reason is your personal discomfort at delegating or whether the person actually lacks the ability to be successful at a task. If it is the latter, and if the associate has received all the appropriate training required, then you have to consider improving the quality of the person occupying the position. Remember that it is a manager's responsibility to assure that team members have proper training before you consider replacing them.

Question 6 - Are your team members the most capable and talented people you can afford to hire?

As a manager you cannot meet objectives if you don't surround yourself with the best people you can afford to hire for the position. Look for the best candidates. Don't fall prey to the idea that a candidate is overqualified and won't stay. Understand instead that if you can't generate additional opportunity or responsibility for a qualified candidate within two years, then you should expect to lose him. Meanwhile, you will have had the benefit of that person's skills and capabilities for two years while generating results and success together.

Question 7 - Do you believe any team members are qualified to succeed you?

The point here is simple. A manager won't move up in responsibility until there is someone in place to succeed him or her. This is the perfect defense for hiring the best people you can afford.

Question 8 - Are any of your staff too weak to enable you to achieve the success you were hired to develop?

This may appear to be a selfish thought, but answering this question really supports your company's decision to hire you. The first question to ask is whether the staff has been properly trained to perform the work. If the answer is affirmative, the next question becomes, Does the individual have the ability to perform the work? The day you enjoy terminating people is probably the day you need to find something else to do. However, your managerial obligation to your employer is to build a team that can generate the results necessary to grow the business.

Question 9 - How effectively and objectively do you evaluate the performance and development of your individual team members?

Most companies have a standard annual performance review that consists of checking boxes on some graduated level. The most important portion of the review, however is the blank section usually labeled "Additional Comments." This is where a world-class manager identifies strengths and weaknesses and documents them, indicates constructive criticism as appropriate, but most important, creates plans for improvement.

Question 10 - Have you initiated individual action plans for team members' development?

These plans are your contract with team members to develop improved performance to generate results and success. It is every world-class manager's responsibility, regardless of the level in the organization, to develop and manage mutually agreed-to plans for each direct report.

Question 11 - Have you been reluctant to reach out and to hire the most talented people you can afford?

Do not be intimidated by talent. If you surround yourself with talented people and manage them effectively, they will make you successful, and you will be credited for developing a world-class team.

In The Wake Of Disaster...Do You Have A Plan?

By Curt Barry

Who would have thought Florida would be hit by four major hurricanes in a few weeks time this past Hurricane Season? When something this devastating occurs, it demonstrates just how important it is to have a plan in place. You have to be ready for the unexpected.

If you think something like this can't happen to your business, think again. Here are a few stories of direct marketing industry companies that were hit with disasters – and survived thanks to having a disaster plan in place before the disaster event occurred.

2004 Hurricane Season: When the staff at Global Response, a call center in Margate, FL, saw the weather reports indicating that Hurricane Frances might be headed their way, they sprung into action. "We immediately set up conference calls with our clients to notify them in advance of our contingency plans in case of the weather," recalls Barbara Turner, director of operations. "We had a document for each client indicating what they wanted us to do in the event that we experienced any weather-related difficulties."

Being based in Florida, Global Response says it has always maintained a Disaster Plan, including a Command Team of key employees in the operations and IT departments who were on-call and meeting several times each day during the crisis. In addition, a Volunteer List was established, comprised of staff people who were willing to stay on site at the call center and work around the clock during the storm.

For many staff people, this was actually a blessing, says Turner, who explains, "Our facility is actually a designated shelter, and many of our staff people live in mobile homes. So we welcomed them to stay on site and even bring their families to work. We had other employees who volunteered to run day care and entertain the kids since the schools were closed."

Adds company CEO Herman Shooster, "Our buildings are like a fortress. None of our technology is on the perimeter, so all of the operations are safe. And there is food and water for all the staff inside. It is a safe place for everyone to remain during the storm."

Though Global Response never experienced any outages during the September storms, Frances, or Jeanne--which also impacted the area later that same month – the company is pleased with how well it came through the disaster. It received several complimentary calls and e-mails from catalog clients and even received flowers from one client. Global Response says the bottom line was its customers were pleased that that it stayed on top of the situation and kept them informed during a difficult time.

Winter Snowstorm: In February of last year heavy snowfall on the East Coast caused the roof to collapse on a roughly 80,000-square foot section at ClientLogic Marketing and Communications' Dover, DE, facility. The company immediately established a recovery team to evaluate the damage and set up a command center at the Dover Sheraton Hotel to keep employees informed as to the developing situation, the Dover Post reported.

Earthquakes Rock the West: It was in 2001 that an earthquake measuring 6.8 on the Richter scale rocked the Seattle area, causing power outages and some damage to area businesses. Recreational Equipment Inc. (REI) catalog, for instance, went without electricity for several hours, according to Catalog Age magazine. The fact that the company had a backup generator for its Web site meant online business could continue without interruption. However, Help Desk staff had to evacuate while the building was being checked for damage, so a message went out that operators were temporarily unavailable to assist customers due to an earthquake.

But not all companies are as ready for disaster as these companies were. In fact, more than one-third of the world's leading companies report they are not sufficiently prepared to protect top revenue sources, according to the 2003 Protecting Value Study. In addition, 100 percent of the companies surveyed report a major disruption to a top revenue source would have a negative impact on earnings, with 28 percent stating such an event would threaten business continuity.

The study, by commercial and industrial property insurer FM Global, the Financial Executives Research Foundation and the National Association of Corporate Treasurers (NACT), polled nearly 400 CFOs, treasurers and risk managers at U.S. and international companies across a variety of industries. Among the other findings of the second annual study:

- 80% of companies report no significant shift in their risk management outlook post-9/11, either strategically or operationally.

- 88% of financial executives say their companies' level of preparation to recover from a major disruption to a top revenue source is "less than excellent."

- 59% of the companies participating in the study report the greatest impact on revenue sources would derive from property-related hazards, including fire or explosion, natural disaster, terrorism, theft, mechanical or electrical breakdown, service disruption, a supply shortage, labor strike or cyber crime.

This last threat brings up an important point to note: Nowadays, you must also add in the Internet risks such as viruses, worms, spam and intentional hackers. Therefore, strategies that protected your company from disaster 10 years ago may not be sufficient today. You must review your Disaster Recovery Plan and see if it has stood the test of time and takes into consideration all of the current technological possibilities.

Another urgent message to companies is you have to practice your Disaster Recovery Plan. Ask yourself, is it executable? Has your plan been updated periodically? Only if you check it regularly and test it will you know it is going to work when you really do need it one day in an emergency situation.

Developing Your Corporate Dashboard Of Key Performance Metrics

By Curt Barry

Introduction

Consider the hundreds of reports and millions of data elements that are generated in your business by merchandising, marketing, fulfillment and financial systems. From all that data, what are you using to run your catalog? What are the key performance metrics, indicators or dials that tell management about customer satisfaction, whether you're on sales plan, how current your inventory is, what your cash flow needs will be, etc.?

Coming up with effective management reports has always been a challenge. This may sound like Catalog Management 101, but we are constantly surprised that this seemingly fundamental aspect of the business is being ignored by many catalogs. As companies grow and continue to add new channels and titles, benchmarking and weekly reporting are key to helping top management keep a finger on the pulse of the business without micro-managing.

One concept worth exploring is the "corporate dashboard" – a series of dials in the corporate cockpit-that reflects the key performance metrics from each department. How can your catalog benefit? By improving customer service, achieving sales and profitability. What are the essential elements to implementing this highly refined online reporting?

What is a Corporate Dashboard?

By dashboard we mean, key indicators of performance in customer service, sales tracking and profitability. When highly summarized, they give management an accurate and timely picture of the business. In order to do this, the information systems also need to provide detail answers (drill down) as to why the various indicators or dials are reporting what they're reporting. Also, as you think through these dials you need to determine which need to be plans, projection and/or actual.

Here are some dials we see in catalog dashboards or weekly reporting:

- From a marketing perspective for the current active catalogs-the demand dollars to date, revenue dollars per catalog for house file and prospect lists separately and in total, average order in units and dollars, order forecast by week, etc.

- From Internet data, total sales generated, unique visitors, total new customers, shopping cart abandonment rate, inventory out of stock, sales per marketing effort (organic search, paid search, e-mail, shopping portals, banner ads, affiliate marketing, etc.).

- Merchandising dials may include category projections, top 20 and bottom 20 selling products, cancellation and return rates in total, high reasons for return products, etc.

- Inventory Control indicators might show initial customer order fill rates compared to item fill rates for the year, summaries of cost recovery and margin loss by liquidation media, summary of initial coverage of products/SKUs as new catalogs mail, etc.

- Customer Contact Center indicators may be limited to call and order activity by channel, call to order ratio, summary of inquiries/complaints and service indicators such as time to answer and call abandonment rate.

- In the Fulfillment Center in-bound receipts and receipts requiring buyer or vendor attention; aging of customer back orders; pick/pack error statistics, order and return turnaround times, packages shipped, etc.

- Finance may report sales actual to plan, summarized cash flow and days to refund/credit customers

One can obviously argue that a dashboard should include or exclude specific dials. There is no one way or standard to implement this as it will vary by management's specific hot buttons, the importance of multi-channels and the ability to report in detail at all levels of management.

Additionally, weekly reporting will obviously differ from monthly reporting. On a monthly basis more formal analysis points are taken (e.g. profit & loss statement, inventory turnover calculated, etc.).

There is a wealth of information in our catalog businesses. What specific dials will give a complete picture of your business?

Three Examples

While many catalogs have not formalized their key performance metrics, leading catalog companies have moved beyond reporting to online management systems that integrate the results of information systems across the enterprise into highly refined dials, graphs and bar charts that are easy to read and interpret.

To better understand what other catalog leaders are doing with corporate performance reporting, here are three examples:

Company A with sales over $1 billion annually-including retail stores, 10 specialty catalog titles and the Internet-has developed an online system that displays all the key business indicators daily. Some indicators are obviously kept as weekly, monthly, catalog-to-date and by season. Sales from the retail stores are downloaded automatically each hour. Every five (5) minutes, phone and Internet order management systems report the number of orders and dollars, average order of sales check by channel. The fulfillment system reports every five (5) minutes on in-bound receipt status and packages shipped. A 52-week history of initial customer order fill rates are reported vs. initial item fill rates as a measure of customer service.

Company B has overlaid its fulfillment, marketing and financial reporting systems with a financial reporting package that uploads key metrics on a daily, weekly and monthly basis. Some of the data is displayed online as well as key metrics reporting.

Company C has implemented departmental operational statistics reporting throughout the company. Marketing, merchandising, call center, fulfillment center and finance managers are responsible for maintaining departmental reports. Departments are also responsible for data integrity, timeliness and accuracy and then extracting and reporting the key daily, weekly and monthly metric. While Company A and B require a significant investment for purchasing a commercial system or developing in-house programming, Company C's model is one that we recommend all catalogs implement.

Detailed Departmental Reporting Key

No matter what approach you take to develop your dials, detailed departmental reporting is essential both to providing key performance metrics at an executive level and being able to break down more detailed statistics when necessary. Let's take for example metrics that are provided to the weekly management team reporting (above) by the director of a Customer Contact Center. The detailed Customer Contact Manager's departmental reporting typically covers 25 to 35 measures of inbound orders, call and non-order activity; outbound contacts and correspondence; performance service levels and cost per contact, call and order. Data integrity, timeliness and accuracy, which are at the heart of this effective reporting, should remain the responsibility of the director of the Customer Call Center.

What are the Benefits?

There is an old industrial engineering principle that says, "What hasn't been measured can't be improved." Establishing this principle will push each of the departments to improve their analysis and internal reporting of efficiency, cost and customer service. One of the most beneficial results that will come from this is "benchmarking internally against yourself" season to season and year to year. Through continual process improvement, your organization will improve internally.

Start Realistically

If you're not reporting key performance benchmarks, start out on a small scale. Reduce it to the essentials and the build on it. Don't get overwhelmed with how many things you could report. Be cognizant of data integrity, timeliness and consistency. If you don't, the process will not be maintainable.

Set realistic benchmarks (internal and external) by exchanging benchmarks and best practices with other. External benchmarking plays an important role in the development of these concepts. While businesses vary dramatically, there are certain foundational benchmarks and best practices that are always important. These external benchmarks are obtained through exchanging ideas with other catalogs and trade organizations.

Conclusion

In this period of uncertainty, there is no better way to improve your catalog's performance-customer service, achieving sales and profitability-than implementing a corporate dashboard of key performance metrics.

15 Expense Saving Ideas

By Curt Barry

In today's world of constantly looking for ways to improve the company's bottom line, many Operations are being asked to reduce costs or better yet, increase productivity and efficiency and lower cost at the same time. Here are 15 areas to look at.

Contact Center

Agent Scheduling

Scheduling agents in the customer contact center can be a very complex task. Contact centers do a good job setting a schedule based on projected call volumes and filling the schedule with available agents, but what happens afterwards? This is where a gap occurs between the schedule and what actually happened. Take time to review the original schedule against the actual volume of calls and agents that worked. This simple task will provide insight into effectiveness of the schedule. The ROI on scheduling software shows that those that have it see their costs lowered.

Organizational structure

As business ebbs and flows, organizational structures tend to remain in tack for long periods of time. This could be an optimal time to review your organizational structure. The web is playing a large part in contact centers today. Internet orders average 35% of total orders with many businesses over 50% now. If internet growth is 20% a year, do you require the same number of full time agents as you did a year ago? Can you use more part time agents? Does this affect your supervisor to agent ratio? 1:20 is a good supervisor to agent ratio.

Off-Phone Work

Off-phone work in the customer contact center has increased over the years with internet growth, email and the use of chat. Many off-phone tasks in the contact center have evolved into major projects. Internet orders containing customization, special instructions and/or customer comments are typically handled in an off-line fashion because they require special handling. Maintaining product information on the order management system is a critical component used to provide great customer service, but in many companies the process of updating this information has been pushed into the contact center. While many of these tasks have evolved into necessity, analyzing the various types of off-phone work will expose unnecessary steps being performed by the agents.

Product training and Company Policy

Product training is becoming a complex undertaking as merchants are constantly searching for new product. With multi-title, multi-channel and a large breadth of SKU's available, keeping agents informed of the latest product information is a challenge. Contact centers that provide regular product training through an established formal training program benefit when the customer places an order. Agents who are not well trained on the product will have to ask for assistance which can lengthen the call time. Large centers have a full time trainer. Public information shows that Cabela's, the world's largest outfitter, has 235,000 SKU's online. Along with product training and product information, communicating important messages to agents is a must. Providing pop-up windows to agents at login time provides an effective communication tool to relay information on problem products and important company meetings. Using online features for customer company policies provides easy and fast access for agents.

Call Monitoring

Monitoring agents and providing feedback on a regular basis is essential to maintaining optimum performance in the contact center. It also provides an opportunity for supervisors to hear what the customer is saying and how the agent interacts with the customer. The use of monitoring is helpful in determining agents strengths, weaknesses and overall efficiency. Monitoring feedback by the supervisor can be used for performance review to increase productivity. Monthly call monitoring by management and merchants is a great way to stay in tune with the customer.

Universal Agents

Universal agents, those that can answer order calls, respond to emails and handle customer service functions are an asset to your organization. These agents are capable of switching tasks as the workload requires maximizing their productivity. Utilizing universal agents, particularly at off-peak times, reduces the need for dedicated agents. A mix of universal and dedicated agents within the contact center provides a balanced workforce that reduces costs and increases efficiency. The use of universal agents makes it tough to track actual work performed and costs associated with each task for benchmarking purposes.

Inventory

Backorders

One of the top customer inquiries and complaints is "Where is my backorder?" The backorder not only costs customer service the time to answer the inquiry, it also costs to ship the product once it arrives in the distribution center. With the cost of a backorder ranging from $7 to $12 per backordered unit of merchandise, it doesn't take long for them to add up and those costs come right off the bottom line. Analyze backorders and improve the accuracy of inventory forecasting. The ROI occurs for a more advanced forecasting system in 12 to 18 months based on reduction in backorders and improved turnover. Customer order fill rate should be reviewed and improved without being out of stock or overstocked. Example of backorder costs: A typical catalog with a 20% backorder rate averaging two items per order processed 200,000 orders for a total of 400,000 units of merchandise. Calculated at 20%, 40,000 customer orders had backorders. Estimating backorder cost on the low end at $7.37 per order, the catalog will have to absorb $294,800 to make up for backorders.

Distribution

Slotting

An ongoing program of determining the correct picking slot locations is a must. Consideration should be given to product velocity (sales) and size (cube) in placing it in the pick line. Having as a goal the storage of at least one weeks average unit movement in the pick slot along with providing a variety of slot sizes should be a key focus.

Picking

There are many picking methodologies to choose from, batch picking, zone picking, pick and pass, pick to cart and pick to box just to name a few. By analyzing the type of product and the type of orders (single vs multi), the most efficient pick path processing can be created reducing travel time. Separating fast movers from slow movers and establishing a "Hot Pick" area for extremely fast movers should be considered. Picking rates range 115 to as high as 180 units per hour.

Packing

If you are not doing pick to box does your system have the capability to determine the box size for the packer? Is the pack station clean, neat and ergonomically setup? Is the appropriate dunnage inserted into each box? Where is the pack verify performed? These are just a few of the questions to look at when analyzing the pack area. Remember, presentation to the customer is as important as getting the shipment out of the door quickly. Packing rates average 35 to 40 per hour.

Inbound Freight

Inbound freight is one of the most overlooked areas for significant cost reduction in many companies. Multichannel companies often spend from 2% to 4% of gross sales on inbound freight. Most successful companies who have paid attention to inbound freight view inbound freight management as controlling inventory in transit. Since inventory is, in many cases, your largest asset, the management of this asset is critical to your business success. There is a growing trend to use freight collect rather than prepaid freight. Inbound freight should be bid out competitively often. Tracking inbound freight receipts and scheduling frees up the dockyard and provides the opportunity to schedule receiving personnel when needed.

Outbound Freight

One of the largest expense items that is always a primary target for cost reduction is outbound freight. With shipping carrier increases in the range of 3% to 5% annually, this is the first area to get questioned, "What can we do to reduce our shipping charges?" In a typical catalogue company, outbound freight ranges 8% to 12% of net sales. Competitively bid out outbound freight often to ensure the best pricing. Combining inbound and outbound freight with one carrier may produce savings. Many multi-channel companies use shipping and handling charges to offset the cost of outbound freight and package handling. Some have grown dangerously close to 20% of net sales.

Replenishment

Insuring that sufficient product is available when the picker needs it ranks as one of the most common warehousing rules that is frequently broken. A combination of scheduled replenishment of the primary pick slot using the min-max and demand replenishment concepts should be employed to increase the likelihood that product is available when needed. If product is not available for the picker, the order is set aside for resolution. This
creates inefficient productivity.

Vendor compliance program

Everything starts at the receiving door of the warehouse. Every function from receiving to shipping is impacted in some way by your vendors. A detailed and enforced Vendor Compliance Program will do as much to improve the warehouse operations as anything you can do. Vendor compliance means that product arrives from a vendor as it should – in proper condition and delivered in the agreed-upon manner. In addition to product quality, compliance standards that vendors must

meet include packaging and shipping requirements, advanced shipping notices, master case and inner case, case labeling, product packaging and polybag specifications, accounting and paperwork requirements, logistics requirements and routing guides, and scheduling and
statistical sampling requirements, to name just a few.

Benchmarking – KPI's

Benchmark, benchmark, benchmark. The best indication of how your
operations is performing is through benchmarking. By developing a
set of consistent and measurable Key Performance Indicators (KPI's),
you can measure your costs, productivity and efficiency. Once you've
completed and analyzed your existing operation, you will want to
compare yourself to accepted industry benchmarks. You want to avoid
using general industry averages as those won't be specific to your
business in product type, size and customers. Many companies are
utilizing management reporting online for critical KPI's for contact
center and fulfillment. You can't improve activities which have not
been measured.

Multichannel Product Pricing

By Curt Barry

It's been less than a decade since the word "multichannel" came into use to describe selling through more than one medium. But the complex new world of multichannel merchandising includes potential pitfalls that at best may confuse customers and at worst will alienate them. Chief among these pitfalls: maintaining different strategies and tactics for different channels.

For instance, a sales representative from one of the country's top office products retailers made a call to our office in Richmond, VA, to invite us to participate in its business account program. The rep said our company was among the top 10 purchasers at the local store. The program includes a separate business catalog with discounted prices for business accounts and free overnight shipping; it also offers monthly billing and allows participants to order online or via phone.

It sounded good, but in shopping for a specific product, we found that prices differed in the store, in the business account catalog, on the Internet, and via the business account contact center. We generally did not find the business account to be the lowest price, and you can't get a business discount with your account at a retail location. One problem could be that the store managers view this program as a threat, thinking it will "steal" top customers. (Although the manager of our local store, when asked about the corporate program, had no idea of what we were talking about.)

Experiences like this, which are all too common in the multichannel world, make customers feel that they must shop across or investigate all possible channels to be assured of getting the best price. Not only is this frustrating, but it deflates a customer's confidence in a company.

Shopping study

To assess how widespread product numbering and pricing differences across channels is, we conducted a survey of 25 major retailers for 145 products on April 4 and 5, both at their stores in Richmond and on their Websites.

The Multichannel Product Pricing chart (at end of article) shows the results of the survey. For 42% of the items, the item number on the store price tag did not match the Website product number — or we couldn't find the in-store item on the Website at all. For Web searches, we started by searching product category, vendor, or designer, then drilling down to item, color, and size. Then we visually matched the image on the Web to what we remembered and had noted in the store.

We were able to find an identical cross-channel match for 47% of the products — in other words, those items had identical product numbers and prices online and in the store. The remaining 11% of the products had some difference in price. Five of these 16 products had price differences of less than $1.00; these are probably errors.

We started shopping in the retail stores with the assumption that the Web would generally have a larger product assortment than the stores. Some merchants (Bath & Body Works, Best Buy, Coldwater Creek, Office Max, and Staples) promotionally priced products at retail and/ or online. It was very easy to find the identical product on the Web for Best Buy, Crate & Barrel, Lowe's, Office Max, Staples, Sur La Table, and Williams-Sonoma simply using the product number to search.

At www.JCPenney.com, if you purchased more than one of an item (such as a cotton duck slipcover) you received a combo discount of $59.99-$149.99 each. Yet there was no in-store signage indicating the promotion, though an item might have been promotionally priced in the store at the point of sale. In fact, in the Eddie Bauer store the salesperson offered to price-match if we found a store item priced differently in its catalog or on its Website.

But playing catch-up by price-matching won't prevent the sort of frustration we witnessed at a major home decor chain, where two women who had researched the product on the Internet had come into the store only to find the bin empty. This raises the question of how retailers can help keep cross-channel shoppers from wasting their time and blaming it on the retailer. Might this sort of problem lead to online inventories by store, for instance?

Open channels

The good news is that the Internet is open. And the bad news is that the Internet is open. As technology has become more sophisticated, shoppers in general have also become much more savvy. They now have a serious tool to help comparison-shop.

Years ago many national retailers preferred to keep their prices consistent: One item, one price, except perhaps where they had to be regionally competitive. Some people we spoke to feel that fewer than 50% of the retailers out there are single-price companies, and that guesstimate is certainly borne out by the sample shopping survey conducted for this article. Yet consumers are still encouraged to look at major retail brands as one company, not different channels or separate businesses.

In a way, customers' ability to do fairly sophisticated comparison-shopping would seem to demand much more synchronization between retail and direct channels. Yet one large apparel catalog and Internet business with whom we spoke says that it intentionally has different prices for the same products sold through multiple titles and business names: In catalog A an item might sell for $39.95, while the identical item may sell for $42.95 in catalog B. Evidently customers have failed to notice the differences. The company also feels that customers do not recognize that the titles are owned by the same parent.

There are several logical reasons for operating with price differences between channels. A retailer may choose to liquidate goods in one channel but not in the other, or it may want to conduct A/B split testing, or it may opt for competitive retail pricing in a particular geographic area. Certain promotions may be more effective in one channel than another, or there may be higher margins in one channel over another.

Software directions

Another reason that many multichannel merchants don't provide consistent pricing may be that they simply don't have the systems to help them do so across media channels and organizational silos. To date there does not appear to be any retail or direct software systems that offer the complete answer to cross-channel item numbering and pricing. Retail-oriented solutions have functions that are effective in pricing and markdown systems at store levels but are light in terms of catalog, drop, source code, versioning, etc. Conversely, direct-oriented solutions lack the ability to handle information by retail region and by store. In terms of internally developed systems, this kind of sophistication is a development priority for the larger multichannel businesses.

Direct software vendors Ecometry and CommercialWare say they are moving toward solutions that will allow all channels to have the same systems and business rules for item pricing and accommodating multiple-item numbering.

Jane Cannon, chief operating officer of Natick, MA-based CommercialWare (which was acquired earlier this year by Datavantage Corp.), describes the CommercialWare pricing engine under development as centralized and stand-alone. This solution will "define pricing [and] track, monitor, and react to multichannel prices across the channels," she says. "There will be four levels of price configuration and hierarchy: global [across the chain and channels], by channel, by category, and by store. This design will cover both stores and direct. 'Category' is meant to accommodate both types of stores — by sales volume such as A,B, or C stores, or by urban/suburban/rural — and catalog version and drop. It will work on an exception basis to minimize the maintenance and input involved." The engine will also include analytics to help users understand the effects of pricing decisions and plan the future on units sold by price point. CommercialWare's beta testing is scheduled for Fall 2006.

Brian Dean, vice president of strategy and marketing for Delray Beach, FL-based Ecometry, says that "the heart of Ecometry's advanced system will be the configuration rules across the chain, Web, and catalog, with the essential marketing and pricing functions inherent to the channel." Ecometry's pricing engine, designed to serve both retail and direct channels, is scheduled to be released in version 9.0 of Ecometry in late July.

Customer cross-channel shopping brings up several thorny tactical questions for multichannel retailers, Dean says. For instance, how does your selling price change if the customer orders on the Internet (or via catalog) and picks it up at a local store? If the business model is that the customer pays when he picks it up, and he adds items while in the store, how does this potentially change your selling prices? Will you honor a price on the Internet at store level? Do you adopt the price book of the store where the customer is shopping? Will there be a best-price guarantee? Will you require pay on pick-up or pay on ordering?

A possible dream?

What does it take to develop consistency between channels? Obviously having a single system of record for multiple channels is a strategy at the heart of the multichannel business of the future.

At the moment, however, many companies manage retail and direct channels separately. Likewise, their systems, policies, and processes are also often organized and conducted in silos. While we don't see separate management going away, it will eventually be imperative for management to think like customers and to view the business as one rather than separate channels.

Some of the basic system requirements for consistent cross-channel pricing and product numbering include providing visibility across the retail chain and across all channels. Merchants will have to reconcile data differences between the channels.
Any solution must also deal with the realities of pricing inherent in each channel, recognizing the complexities of retail pricing related to discounting and mass-merchandising. Item pricing across channels must be rules based.

In short, you need to decide on a strategic corporate philosophy as seen from the customers' point of view. And you need to develop a customer service policy to take care of customers when they bring up cross-channel pricing, whether in the form of downright errors, competitive pricing, or the effort they've put into cross-channel shopping research.

Tips to minimize pricing pitfalls

If a customer complains about a difference in pricing between what he paid and the reduced retail price within 14 — or even 30 — days following a sale, give a credit or a refund.

Get the direct channels (catalog and Internet) in sync with each other as a first priority. Tightly integrate your order management systems to the Internet and the catalog. Then over time integrate campaign management and pricing among all channels.

When preparing an e-mail blast promoting markdowns, try to suppress customers who have just purchased products at full price.

Develop an IT strategy so that channels use the same systems and business rules for item price, item numbering, shipping and handling tables, and value-added services. Obviously there will need to be exceptions for the logical times when pricing really needs to differ by channel.

If you don't offer uniform pricing across channels, remember to have your returns staff look up the selling price when returns come back into the store or the distribution center without an order number or a receipt.

With direct returns, retailers will want to attribute the return back to the original order and the channel.

How To Develop A Cost Effective, Customer Service Oriented Shipping Strategy

By Curt Barry

The direct to customer industry (catalog and Internet) finds itself at a cross roads in terms of shipping & handling policies and charges.

Item: Many catalogs report a growing frustration by consumers with shipping & handling charges. Some studies show consumers are refusing to place the order if the S&H charges are perceived to be out of line with the competition. However, shipping & handling is a necessity and often represent 8% to 10% of a catalog's average order and net sales to offset some of the pick and pack labor, outbound freight charges and packing materials. Shipping & handling is one of the top 5 business expenses.

Item: Expedited carriers UPS and FedEx have routinely announced rate increases of 3.5% annually. However, the actual charges experienced by catalogs may be considerably higher because residential surcharges, rural delivery and other accessorial charges increased considerably more than this average. USPS Priority Mail last increase took away a low cost way to ship packages under 3 pounds.

Item: There have been several class action suits against catalogs over shipping & handling. As we write this article, there is a controversial "white paper" being prepared by a direct marketing industry organization which calls excessive S&H charges "which are not reasonable" -

unethical.

What to do about S&H, how to decrease costs and increase service is one of the major challenges to the direct to customer industry. Given the seriousness of these issues, it is imperative that catalog owners and executives give developing a cost effective, customer service oriented shipping strategy their highest priority.

Getting Organized

Establish a project team

Shipping strategies shouldn't be just the domain of fulfillment. Set up a team with members from Marketing, Customer Service and Sales. While only one person will serve as the lead negotiator, get the ideas, buy in and requirements of the entire organization which when combined will give customer service, sales and marketing competitive advantage.

Know your business model's shipping characteristics

Develop a profile of your outbound shipping including the number of marketing orders, shipped orders, packages shipped, back order rates, ship alone, historical order and package shipped volumes by month with seasonal peaks and valleys, etc. The level of service used (e.g. next day, 2 day or ground) and why; zone distribution, weight distribution; number of business, residential, rural or urban deliveries. What will be your growth projections by year for three years? Do your homework and dig out the facts – many times there are assumptions made which prove flawed and change the actual versus budgeted costs. The carrier will have their own data collection forms but these are the types of data the carriers will use to develop your pricing proposal and estimate their profitability. By analyzing this data, you may also determine the opportunities for improvement. For example, catalogs are putting more emphasis on forecasting and inventory management and initial order fill rate to better serve the customer and also reduce back order costs.

Determine customer presentation and packing requirements

From a customer perspective, is there a marketing advantage or image that you want to communicate to the customer (e.g. FedEx versus a mail box delivery)? Is one carrier more liberal with free packing materials than another? Are there some options that the carrier offers that will decrease breakage?

Determine your delivery service requirements

From our experience and customer surveys, we have always felt that it was important to have the package in office or home within 7 days unless a more expedited plan was requested. We think with the changes in rates and services, to ask your self if you are over servicing the customer's expectations. The important thing is to deliver on what you promise in terms of delivery dates. Are there other expectations which can be adjusted without damaging the relationship or losing the sale? How flexible are you - are you open to switching to alternate vendors and methods?

Fulfillment closer to your customers

What's your fulfillment strategy? Especially in multi-channel retail/direct companies, if you are also expecting to expand your fulfillment capabilities, look at whether multiple centers or a move more to your customer's demographic center, will place you closer to pockets of customers and cut down delivery zones, times and costs. Or can you locate a new center at a hub which would allow a much later cut-off on order processing times and fill a higher percent of same day shipped orders. Reduction in shipping costs by relocation is a major element in the return on investment of many fulfillment centers.

Do your homework about carriers and pricing

Understand the value/importance of your business to the carriers

Many catalogs are in less densely populated areas and often represent major volume. Will your business qualify as a national or key account? What are the local market conditions and competition for volume?

Educate yourself on pricing and negotiating tactics of carriers

As with any service, the differences in how vendors price adds another element to getting "an apples to apples" comparison. Here are a few examples. Undeliverable packages are returned free of charge by UPS whereas FedEx charges a 3 day rate for air returns. Does one carrier discount residential over another? "Rural" surcharges vary by carriers but are assessed even in high population urban centers (e.g. high crime areas). FedEx separates pick up by service level for residential, commercial and air/international. Learning how carriers charge and what's discountable and negotiable is critical.

Know where the "hidden" and accessorial costs are

Hundred weight service, over size/dimensional packages, per package pricing, residential and rural surcharges, master packing or shipment pricing options, declared value coverage, carrier guarantee waivers, service failure refunds, address corrections, minimum per package charges. A carrier's proposal may list the pricing for these charges but your analysis will understate these charges without a thorough analysis of your freight bills.

Obtain and study carrier management reports

Carriers are typically not going to offer these to you unless you ask for them. There's a treasure trove of information about your account contained in the carrier management reports. But you have to know what to ask for and how to use them. They generally show year to date package volume, billings (revenue) by month this year and last year. Another key data point is the revenue per package shipped from which the carrier will judge their profitability.

Get the credits due your company

It's getting harder and harder to collect on errors from carriers. However, we recommend setting up a program to audit freight bills and service failure refunds. Understand that carriers may negotiate out your ability to audit their bills electronically by limiting the size of batches or reducing discounts. There are other specialists which will work on a gain share basis to achieve savings.

Determine where do the various methods and plans fit into your strategy

Small package carriers, LTL, truck load, air freight, consolidators and USPS – where do they fit into your strategy? Is there an opportunity to leverage inbound and outbound strategies with the carriers?

Integrate electronically with your carriers

Now a days, the carrier's expectations are that you will integrate electronically to their systems through FedEx Powership, FedEx MC, UPS Worldship system, Accuship, "best way" rate shopping and EDI billing solutions. Some catalogs still provide system printouts of shipped packages which have to be rekeyed into the carrier systems. This can be expensive in terms of errors, delays and carrier costs passed on to you.

Implement web tools and the Internet

There are a wide variety of web based tools to assist your customer service shipping and tracking. These include shipping cost calculators, package tracking systems, on-line reporting of shipping activity and carrier management, system alerts of weather, delays, etc. Through your Internet site give your customers the ability to track their packages reducing call center service requirements.

Selecting the carrier

Request For Proposal

With your project team, determine order, shipped and return package volume growth projections by year for three years and your shipping characteristics. Should the proposal address inbound as well as outbound freight? What service level plans? Give the carrier a specific format you want the RFP answered in. Request the payment terms, response date and sample agreement. From your existing carrier you can generally get an impact statement of how their proposed rates will increase your costs because they will have the detail shipping characteristics.

Carrier Selection

You need to take your RFP questions and design a decision matrix to get an "apples to apples" comparison of the vendor responses. Carriers will not answer the questions in an orderly way that will allow easy comparison from a pricing perspective. Generally they will give you a price list. You need to develop a pro-forma cost by year including all the "hidden costs" and accessorial costs for the expected contract life.

Consider using a transportation consultant

As we said at the outset, shipping & handling strategy and costs is a rough and tumble area of catalog operations. Whatever you thought you knew and negotiated two years ago has changed dramatically. Consider hiring an expert to assist in the negotiations of carrier rates, service, audits of freight bills, etc. We all want to believe that we are good at negotiating the best deals for our companies. What we have found is that often there is more room for savings when an expert is involved. These specialists know the recent competitive and market developments; they can determine the net effective rates based on actual shipping characteristics; they know what is discountable; they can analyze the rates and impacts of accessorial charges; they know how to read and interpret carrier management reports; with all of this they can model carrier proposals versus your unique shipping characteristics. Generally these consultants work on a shared savings basis for several years so that there isn't any cost directly for their services. Because they are paid from the savings, the up front cost studies and negotiations are not out of pocket costs. If such an expert can't find sufficient savings, then that's good news. Throw a party because you've achieved the lowest possible costs for the time being on one of your major expenses.

Contact
Center

Reducing Costs In The Contact Center, Conducting A Post Season Analysis

By Tocky Lawrence

As 2007 comes to a close, many of our clients are turning their thoughts to how they can save money — both in their contact centers and throughout their operations — as well as starting to prepare for holiday season 2008. One of the best ways to plan for future success is to conduct a postseason analysis. In this first of a two-part series, I'll explain how to perform a postseason analysis of your center as a baseline for customer service, process improvement and cost reduction.

Here's a step-by-step guide to the postseason analysis.

1. **Form a postseason review team.** Because your efforts are directed at customer service, process improvement and potential cost reduction, form a team that can bring different disciplines to the process. While much of the work will fall to contact center management (managers and supervisors), broaden the group to involve a few good reps. Also include general training and quality training, human resources, center scheduling, telecom traffic, IT, marketing, and returns and replacement if all of these areas are within your responsibilities.

Clearly, contact center management drives the process. But this effort should draw on the opinions and input of all. Challenge them to assess how things could be done differently, and make them answer the question, "How can costs be reduced without lowering customer service?" These meetings should occur sometime between mid-January and mid-February, giving you enough time to plan and achieve early results.

2. Review your metrics. Begin by reviewing your key performance indicators and how performance measures up against your standards and plans. The major metrics include contacts per hour; service level; abandon rate; attrition/turnover rate; call-handle time; talk time; after-call work time; contact-to-order ratio; transaction volumes for Internet, phone and mail; non-phone volumes and others. How accurate were marketing's projections and your projections for calls?

Labor is 50 percent to 70 percent of the contact center's costs. So it's important to see how well you performed in terms of staffing-level accuracy, schedule adherence and occupancy percentage.

3. Review hiring and training practices. Labor's cost, quality and availability is becoming an issue for many call centers, particularly in seasonal businesses where the selling curve is more compressed. Review your advertising media costs and results, and exchange information with other human resource departments. Review your prehiring testing, employee selection criteria and practices. What improvements and cost reductions are possible? Is there a place for temporary agencies rather than relying completely on in-house hiring? Should more calls be shunted off to outsourced call centers?

From a training perspective, how well did you train the CSRs to take orders and provide customer service? In our experience, there's a considerable cost ($3,000 to $10,000 per new hire) and loss of time by senior associates to hire and train new CSRs before they're productive. How can this be improved (number of classes and trainers; develop better training approaches such as e-learning, post-training surveys, length of training)?

4. Evaluate revenue generation. As part of their mission, many contact centers are charged with becoming revenue centers in addition to taking orders and providing customer service. What do your reports show about your success with cross-selling, up-selling, outbound selling and increasing the company's average order?

5. Consider process improvements. What does your quality and call monitoring show about your operation? As you walk through your system and operation, where are the bottlenecks? How can systems be streamlined? What functions and types of information can your system do more easily online? If you're still processing batches of mail orders, can scanning reduce costs? How can live chat and e-mail management systems improve your operation? Do you need to move to the next level of call-scheduling software?

Major Cost Saving Practices

Once you have decided on a post-season review, you will need to assemble a team from across the organization. This team should have fulfillment, merchandising, HR and the contact center represented. Include as many areas of the contact center as possible, from the director, managers, supervisors, traffic/scheduling, training and quality to a few agents who would be open and willing to participate. But remember that any number of participants greater than 12-15 is usually too difficult to manage.

- **Self-evaluation of the contact center management team** is a great starting point. This will work to bring the entire team together and develop trust with the rest of the team members. The team should consider:

- ○ Did you have the right amount of leadership/support staff for the season?
- ○ Was the leadership staff able to assist with most of the issues that developed or arose throughout the season?
- ○ Was the organization's leadership able to support the needs of the contact center for the season?

If the answers to any of these items raise further questions or concerns, you need to evaluate the concern and then work to develop the proper training and support system to be successful in the coming year.

- **Agent adherence and scheduling** is an area that can be a point of contention for the entire organization; how it impacts your service level throughout the seasons is very important to understand. With agent labor being your single greatest expense—anywhere from 60-70% of all contact center expenses—this is mission critical. A simple review of Erlang C and the importance of everybody in their seat at the right time is an ideal starting point. It is also a good idea to review the service levels that have been committed to or assigned to the contact center. If staffing is an issue or if the labor expense is out of line, you might want to rethink your service level. Utilizing a benchmarking service is vital to the success of your metrics. Incorporate comparisons with others to develop greater understanding and see if you are measuring the appropriate standards and are achieving a best-in-breed service. Also try to identify an organization that can provide the needed support when benchmarking. For areas that prove too difficult to handle on your own—and these are inevitable—allowing for a third party to work with you will help to ensure success.

- **Attrition:** It is vital to understand when, where and why your staff is leaving. Challenge HR to help get a handle on this issue. Using pre-hire screening and testing is a great alternative to just taking the first soul with a pulse for the position. It can only benefit the entire organization to have a well-staffed and well-trained workforce.

- **Training program:** Can you make it more beneficial to the agents? Is there waste that needs to be eliminated? It is vital that your training classes are actually training! On the job training is not an efficient or cost effective process to get agents up to speed on your programs. Utilizing an e-Learning program for the basics could be very useful. It will allow you to train consistently, efficiently and, more importantly, it will allow for more focus on role-playing and product knowledge training. Most systems training can be automated. You should engage either a consultant or an instructional designer to assist with training content development. Content is one of the most overlooked and undervalued parts of the process in a contact center, but ultimately, it has the most impact on agents' learning and, as a consequence, their tenure. Spend the time and attention needed to make this successful; it will only benefit the organization in the long run.

- **Outsourcing:** After taking a long, hard look at the results of your post-season review, you may find what you see so discouraging and challenging that you realize it is necessary to outsource the peak business. Don't be ashamed of this! In fact, you should be commended for realizing that there is a place and niche for outsourcing relationships. Now, the challenge is to find the right fit for your organization. It is not as easy as opening the phone book and finding a pizza delivery company. You will need to solicit RFP's from potential outsourcers, make site visits and work through a transition. None of this is for the weak at detail; you will need help. It is a great benefit to have assistance from a consultant to shepherd you through the process. Allow someone else to do the research and present their findings for your review and approval.

- **Voice of the Customer:** The most important questions are, was the customer taken care of and will they return? Implementing a Voice of the Customer program is a great way to assure future success. There are several sources you can use for developing a solid platform on which to work with your customers throughout the year. A third party can do it for you, or you might want to bring in a consultant to assist in the formulation of a VOC program. This is a benchmark that you will want to both develop and keep an eye on throughout the year.

Balancing Your Budget And Investment: When Is The Right Time To Outsource?

By Tocky Lawrence

Many multichannel merchants focus on how they can lower operating costs when they consider outsourcing certain tasks. But when you outsource operations, you also outsource the investment. Sounds obvious, but maybe the magnitude isn't all that clear until you're faced with replacing an order-management system, moving into a new fulfillment space or upgrading your Web site.

When outsourcing your investment, you don't have to invest in those upgrades as your business grows and changes. Let's look at some examples that show the size of these investments.

Order-management systems. Software as a service (SaaS) can free up a potential investment of $25,000 for an emerging company. If you're a $500 million company — with several hundred users adopting a SaaS model — it eliminates an $8 million to $10 million investment. For a $20 million cataloger, the spend runs $280,000 to $400,000 to license and buy hardware. Then you implement an order-management system with call center and warehousing functions.

Specialized forecasting and inventory management system (working in conjunction with your fulfillment system). Here, investment and implementation costs for a 10-user system will cost, on the low end, $150,000. Larger companies invest several million dollars.

Replacing an e-commerce site. SaaS business models can eliminate an investment of $750,000 to $1.2 million for a multichannel cataloger with sales in excess of $100 million. With the e-commerce that growing companies experience, there's also often a need for an e-mail management or chat-system investment.

Call-center operations. Outsourcing eliminates investment in the required space, telecom terminals, headsets, ACD, scheduling software, call-monitoring hardware and software, e-mail management, chat systems, etc.

Fulfillment center. You avoid investing in the construction and/or build-out costs, as well as the racking, conveyors, material handling, warehouse management systems, shipping systems, furniture and fixtures. Plus, you avoid a long-term lease.

It should be pointed out that when looking at these investments on a five- to seven-year basis, many would have been amortized and depreciated over that time. But many companies are struggling to make the initial and ongoing investments because of the competition for financial resources.

Here are some of the questions you need to answer as you look at outsourcing and the business investment:

1. Are you keeping pace with investment in the infrastructure required?
2. What alternatives for capital use does your business have rather than investing in physical assets?
3. Does the outsource provider have the finances to grow and expand? What's its track record of doing this for clients?
4. How will those costs be passed onto your business as it grows and changes?

5. Can a major activity be outsourced and not result in a total loss of control (e.g., call-center overflow, peaks and weekends)?

6. Which provider best understands your category of product (e.g., apparel with its high SKU storage needs, returns, etc.) and mode of operation (e.g., e-commerce, catalog management systems, etc.)?

7. Which provider will be the best long-term partner?

8. How vulnerable will this leave you if the provider's performance isn't up to par?

9. If you wish to sell your business and don't own major assets, does this help you (the prospective owners aren't paying for assets) or hurt you (you may need to remain operationally independent of the other businesses a prospective owner has invested in)?

The Issue of Control

So why isn't outsourcing more commonplace? Most managers want to control their own destiny. Outsourcing means giving up some control.

Also in certain cases, the outsource industry providers have a less than stellar record of long-term, reliable and cost-effective service. Many, including myself, believe that SaaS business models will change much of this. I've also seen many companies successfully use both domestic and offshore call-center facilities. We've had one client outsource all call-center and fulfillment operations for its $25 million apparel catalog and e-commerce business since 1988.

10 Steps To Developing A Successful Third-Party Fulfillment Partnership

By Tocky Lawrence

Most of the direct world uses internal fulfillment. This is a mistake many companies make because they don't think high-quality service levels can be achieved and maintained using third party fulfillment (3PF). The truth is that many companies want to manage their own operations and they are dubious about turning over control to a third party. And yet fulfillment and operations distractions often do not let companies concentrate on marketing and merchandising their businesses which is vital to profitable growth.

Dozens of non-profit businesses use outsourcing because they recognize fulfillment is not a core competency – making a profit funds their mission's activities. Many Holiday season catalogs don't have to recruit, train and staff for a short season when they use 3PF. A multi-warehouse fulfillment strategy may reduce inbound and outbound freight costs. Start-ups should seriously consider outsourcing to avoid capital use for facilities and systems and incur higher fulfillment costs.

Here are ten steps to take toward making a third-party fulfillment partnership successful and profitable:

1. Developing a successful 3PL partnership requires a significant amount of time, effort and follow-up by from the client com-

pany. It is important to immediately identify to all personnel that you have relinquished only the physical handling of your product to the 3PL and not the responsibility for managing your business.

2. Identify the client contacts and decision-makers who will be issuing direction to the 3PL. The 3PL group needs to clearly understand from whom they will receive direction and who their "go to" is to resolve problems.

3. Remember that the 3PL is proud of how it has chosen to manage its business. Conversing with the 3PL requires the same consideration you would extend to your most valued associates inside the client company. Never ignore issues or problems, but be firm and respectful. The 3PL is normally quite aware of who is paying the bills and who owns the inventory. The 3PL exists to serve; be a gracious ruler.

4. Communicate daily with 3PL management and visit the site as frequently as travel restrictions permit. Discuss the basics of the previous day's operations: receiving, shipping, inventory management. Always inquire what you can do to assist them to achieve their goals and objectives. If possible visit monthly, but no less than quarterly. This sort of relationship can be a classic case of "out of sight, out of mind." Your being involved maintains your status in the 3PL's thoughts as a client who is on top of what they are doing and following their performance.

5. As a client you have to be diligent in managing the 3PL through daily reporting. You are now managing a remote location, even if it's in the same community, and therefore your best source of information is the 3PL's daily reporting and invoices. This is no different than managing your own operation. Master the information reporting so you can identify trends and immediately spot

issues as they appear.

6. Inventory management is the most important reporting needed to manage a 3PL. The client has to know where to look for such issues as lost or damaged inventory, or out of stock when the inventory records indicate adequate supply. These are indications of performance issues requiring the client's follow-up and resolution.

7. Receiving performance and inbound scheduling are next in importance for daily follow-up. The client has to know if there are vendor delivery issues or 3PL receiving issues which will negatively impact customer service level.

8. Normal daily shipping follow-up is important, but the most important thing to know is what did not ship.

9. Returns reporting is a critical trend report that enables you to identify not only client satisfaction with your product, but also 3PL performance issues. Detailed reason code reporting is imperative, and cumulative graphing is also valuable in discussions with the 3PL.

10. As a client you have to remain objective and aggressive in your efforts to manage your business reputation through the 3PL. A 3PL by nature of its activity now has more influence over the client's customer's perspective than the client has. Do not become a passive or uninvolved/uninformed client.

With the proper project definition and research you can make this a positive and profitable business decision for you and your customers.

Managing Your Cost Per Call

By Tocky Lawrence

In many areas of the country, the labor costs for CSRs are increasing quickly, and these rates are not going to decrease. Additionally, the quality of the labor pool to draw from is not ideal due to low unemployment rates in many markets. And the direct-to-customer industry is in competition for CSRs with other sectors such as financial services.

The direct industry has a difficult balancing act to perform. On the one hand, we want to provide a high level of customer service—and that's getting tougher each year. On the other hand, the cost of direct labor per hour has increased from less than $7 to more than $11 per hour during the last five years. In some markets rates are well over that, as high as $14 an hour. Benefit costs have also increased, and now average 15% to 20% of pay.

Cost benchmarks

The use of universal agents, increasing Internet order volume, and the need for contact center to support e-mail and online activity all make it more difficult for companies to define their costs clearly. Typically, contact centers measure their cost-per-call, cost-per- contact, and cost-per-order.

We define fully loaded cost-per-call as including direct, indirect, and management labor; benefits, incentive pay, training, recruitment, third-party call center services, correspondence costs, telecommunications, and occupancy. To better understand the cost per call, we reviewed our proprietary benchmarking database, looking at 18 large companies with call volumes ranging from 900,000 to more than 9 million calls annually.

Here are the findings:

- The direct labor cost ranges from $1.11 to $3.29 for a 3-to-4–minute direct consumer call.

- When we add in indirect labor, the cost-per-call increases to a range of $1.39 to $4.75 per call.

- When we add in occupancy, benefits, and telecommunications, the fully loaded costs range between $2.70 to $5.60 per call.

Fully loaded costs for smaller companies would be more in the range $6.00 to $8.00 or higher. (For purposes of this analysis we have left out the cost-per-call credit card processing costs.)

Total fulfillment costs for efficient companies range from $8 to $13 per order, including the major cost elements for contact center and fulfillment (but not including shipping and handling). As the data above show, contact center costs can account for as much as 50% of the cost per order.

10 ways to reduce the cost per call

1. Do you have cost and service level standards that you have set and are trying to perform to? Do you have an actual budget that defines cost per call/order/contact? Remember the industrial

engineering cliché, "You can't improve something you don't measure."

2. Improve scheduling and adherence to the schedule. Improving the schedule will depend on having the right software tools, but much of your success will also depend on management to make sure that people adhere to the schedule.

3. Make better use of part-time workers rather than full-time workers during order-buying peaks and valleys.

4. Increase the in-seat occupancy rate. A high occupancy rate would be 85%–90% after breaks, lunches, and meetings are subtracted.

5. Use call monitoring and improve training and computer literacy. Of course CSRs should be conversant with products and company policies; but they also have to field questions and comments about Websites, browsers, and shopping carts from Internet-savvy customers.

6. Investigate outsourcing. Highly productive outsource providers may be able to guarantee a standard level of service and cost. Is this beneficial to your business? How does it lower your costs? What contractual service levels and costs will make this acceptable?

7. Reduce service levels. The standard is to answer 80% of calls in 20 seconds. Some are experimenting with reducing that to 70% in 30 seconds. Would that be effective in spite of reduced levels of customer service?

8. Reduce the call-to-order ratio. An average ratio would be between 1.2 and 1.4 calls per order for many direct businesses. As Internet

orders increase dramatically in many companies, that ratio decreases to less than 1.0. What are the reasons for the calls? Website ease of use? Catalog copy questions? Where is my backorder? Take action on how to reduce these calls.

9. Can you use IVR for order status checking to reduce customer service calls?

10. Does your on hold message refer customers to your Website if all agents are busy?

The impact of the Internet, direct labor rates, and availability of labor all need to be addressed. The real issue, however, is how well is your contact center being managed? That's the first line of support for your customer.

Third-Party Fulfillment

By Curt Barry

Q: We're thinking about using third-party fulfillment and call center services. How should we go about selecting the vendor?

A: Most of the direct world uses internal fulfillment. Many companies don't think that they can achieve and maintain high service levels using third-party fulfillment (3PF), or they fear that outsourcing will cost more per order. And, of course, many are dubious about turning over control.

But in reality, fulfillment and operations distractions often do not let companies concentrate on marketing and merchandising, which are vital to profitable growth.

Dozens of nonprofit businesses use outsourcing because they recognize that fulfillment is not a core competency. Many seasonal merchants don't want to recruit and train the auxiliary staff needed during their brief peak season. Outsourcing can enable a multi-warehouse fulfillment strategy, which may reduce inbound and outbound freight costs. Start-ups should seriously consider outsourcing to limit their capital expenditures.

If you're considering outsourcing your fulfillment, follow these steps:

1. **Define your requirements.** Start out by understanding your cur-

rent costs. For the contact center analyze your internal cost per contact, call, and order. For back-end fulfillment try to analyze the various departments' functions and their costs. Many vendors invoice at a function level (order processing, returns, backorders, prep time, receiving), so breaking out your current costs this way will enable you to compare vendors' pricing fairly.

2. **Determine the business parameters, metrics, and customer service levels that will be used by the vendors for pricing.** Business parameters include average call length, call and order volumes per month, call-to-order ratio, split rate of multi-box shipments, historical backorder rates, returns percentages, and number of units to be received. You should develop a three- to five-year order projection to use with the vendors.

   In terms of customer service levels and standards, what do you expect of your 3PF? For the contact center you need to define an acceptable abandonment rate, average time to answer, call length, and e-mail turnaround time, among other metrics. For fulfillment you need to specific receiving and quality-assurance standards, picking error rates, inbound shipment receipt to put away times, returns processing times, and percent of orders shipped same day.

3. **Determine the processing functions you expect the 3PF to deliver.** In the contact center, do you expect services other than order-taking and customer service—online chat, for instance, or e-mail handling? Likewise, in the fulfillment center, do you expect the 3PF to handle gift wrapping and personalization, receiving, returns processing, and prep work as well as picking, packing, and shipping?

4. **Assess your current and future information systems needs.** Remember that the outsource service also becomes your IT de-

partment for many functions. Identify your systems needs including order management system , Website development and integration, real-time inventory, inventory purchasing, forecasting, data warehousing, circulation analysis, product category and item analysis of results, and financial reporting. Is their data warehousing robust enough to allow you to extract and analyze your data easily? You need to be sure the vendor's systems are proper for your business. You don't want to customize systems unless absolutely imperative.

5. **Develop the request for proposal (RFP).** One of the gravest mistakes you can make is to try to select a vendor without a detailed RFP and competitive bidding. The vendor responses and costs become the standards content for the contract of the finalist. For example, there will be a significant cost difference for contact center service levels (e.g. 80% calls answered in 20 seconds vs. 70% in 30 seconds). The RFP levels the playing field among vendors and sets forth your expectations.

   When developing the RFP, spell out your operations environment as well as the system functions and reports you expect. Ask the vendor for references, who ideally would be in businesses similar to yours. Have the vendor spell out its implementation methodology and timeframe. Get a sample contract. And don't forget to identify who in your company is responsible for this project and to provide the vendor with a deadline for when the RFP response is due.

6. **Develop a short list of qualified vendors.** Use industry resource guides, conferences, networking, and Web searches to identify potential vendors. Call 3PF providers, talk with them about your

requirements, the types of business they handle (hard goods, collateral, apparel), the number of active clients they have, and the locations of their facilities. You generally don't want to send an RFP to more than five vendors or fewer than three. So do your qualifying and homework up front.

7. **Distribute the final RFP.** Before you send the RFP off to the vendors on your short list, get a sign-off internally that the RFP represents your business's requirements. Once you send out the RFP, allow the vendor two to three weeks to respond. During this time the vendor will likely need to call or e-mail you to clarify certain specifications so that it can provide you with an accurate and realistic response.

8. **Set up a decision-and-cost matrix spreadsheet.** This should allow you to prepare a detailed side-by-side comparison of the short list of vendors. If vendors respond in an incomplete manner, after several tries you should disqualify them. The decision-and-cost matrix should compare pricing, service levels and standards, functions expected, implementation methodology, and systems required to be provided by each vendor. Use a weighting factor to prioritize the functions and features that are most important to your business decision.

9. **Select the finalists.** Select the best two choices after you have validated the responses as best you can over the phone or in person. This should obviously be made based on cost, standards agreed to, system and account management support, transition plan, and the "trust" factor.

10. **Check references and make a site visit.** Work up a standard list of questions you can ask each reference. The vendor will give you its best references, obviously. Ask each vendor for its total client

list, and take the time to follow up. Call as many references as you can for your type of business. For the site visit, plan on spending a day at each finalist's facility. Take your matrix and study materials so that you can ask any necessary questions and validate responses.

11. **Make the final selection.** After the reference calls and the site visit, make sure that you have the finalist respond to any open questions and pricing changes.

12. **Negotiate the contract.** Proposals and verbal representations must be written down and reflected in the contract. Be sure to clearly identify the functions and standards that you expect the provider to perform. Use an attorney who is experienced in this type of law.

Forecasting & Inventory Management

How Well Are You Managing Your Inventory?

By Curt Barry

Inventory is most likely the largest balance sheet asset in your company. How well you plan, purchase, and manage your inventory largely determines your level of customer service and profits.

But selling goods in multiple channels means dealing with channel-specific planning and inventory needs.

Based on our consulting work with clients and observations from conducting the F. Curtis Barry & Co. Inventory ShareGroups, we've come up with some strategies to consider with multichannel inventory management.

Planning and inventory systems

In most companies, the systems for merchandise planning and inventory control remain highly fragmented by channel.

For promotional planning, many multichannel companies need to be more diligent and use a single promotional calendar rather than channel-specific schedules on which merchandise planning is based. These should include in-store promotions, catalogs, and e-mail campaigns.

Detailed channel-level inventory systems cater more to individual channel planning and inventory needs. In retail, assortment planning is performed by merchandise division, department, class, and product/SKU, with another view by region, store level, and product/SKU plans. Large retailers also have store replenishment systems to recommend restocking orders for retail locations.

For most direct companies, assortment planning differs from retail; it's by catalog season, drop, department, class, and product/SKU. The data elements — though similar to retail — have some major differences, using demand, cancellations, returns, space used by category (pages, square inches, depictions), and other direct metrics. Most direct companies have not invested in formalized systems and are using internally developed systems or, more likely, spreadsheets.

Emerging direct businesses with stores don't have comprehensive retail planning systems. Often they can't justify the investment and use spreadsheets or other elementary systems more effectively. But there is a huge potential for sales and profit improvement through better planning.

To get results to flow through corporate planning, inventory and accounting systems, large retail companies identify top level plans, sales and inventory results and display as a store: "catalog store," "Internet store," or maybe the direct business combined as a store.

Many companies have tried to use channel-oriented planning and inventory systems (i.e., retail designed or direct designed) for other channels. But these have been less than successful due to the differences in views of the data (e.g., region and store) and the types of detailed data mentioned above.

Internet inventory management philosophies are slowly evolving in most companies. Traditional catalogers now average more than 50%

of sales from the Internet, although much of that business is generated by receipt of the catalog.

Products may be active and available longer if there is stock. What sells online is heavily influenced by placement on landing pages and organization and ranking within category product searches.

The online product assortment can be more extensive than that in a single catalog. Internet may have a total chain assortment different from any one store or region. The Website may have a clearance or liquidation aspect. These principles of planning and managing inventory are not industry established best practices, but are being hammered out in the trenches every day.

From a purchasing perspective, companies are rolling multiple channel plans and forecasts together into a single purchase order management system to write Pos.

The eventual multichannel inventory system that evolves will be a new animal. It will need to be a blend of channel-specific function (such as store replenishment logic for reorderable product) and direct (such as promotional and time-based elements more like catalog).

It will also have a single inventory system that can be displayed by product/SKU and allow you to see the plan by channel and promotion, vendor on-order and on-hand by store, and warehouse location. The planning modules will remain channel specific.

When will there be true integrated systems for planning and inventory systems? For most companies, not any time soon. Retail and direct channels have different data needs and processes. It will probably be a few years before commercial software companies that cater to retail and direct have the most basic of systems in place. MICROS Retail,

Direct Tech, and Manhattan Associates all have development projects to bring channels together in terms of planning and inventory systems.

Channel Inventory – a distribution view

With all the complexities of planning and inventory control, how are distribution centers accommodating the channels? When multichannel marketing was in its infancy more than a decade ago, the prevalent thinking was to have a single DC that would process both direct and retail replenishment orders. There would be one pooled inventory, one staff and one facility — end of discussion. But logistics thinking is changing.

Looking at the chart "How nine merchants manage distribution" on page 35, the last column on the right shows whether a company dedicates one or more DCs to direct, has separate retail DCs or uses shared facilities between channels.

For example, Companies B and C have multiple distribution centers dedicated to direct orders, and other centers for stores. These two companies' objectives are to shorten the delivery time to the customer and reduce transportation costs to cover the entire country.

But to accomplish this, they have the additional overhead of multiple facilities and staffing, and their warehouse management and order management must be capable of managing multiple inventories and allocating and filling orders.

Adding a second direct DC adds at least 40% more inventory, and sometimes goes even higher. Plus, opening multiple DCs presents a management challenge of transplanting your culture and company philosophy to a totally new group of employees.

As e-commerce in retail companies has grown substantially, logistics management has come to realize that picking, packing, and shipping of small orders is very different from full-carton replenishment to stores. With large volumes it may prove to be more efficient to have dedicated centers for direct.

Company I is a manufacturer with 50 stores and an e-commerce and catalog business unit. It also picks from stores where fast-selling products can be allocated, and the stores ship. The downside to this is that stores are begrudgingly giving up best-selling product. The company's philosophy is to achieve high fulfillment of customer orders, to leverage inventory and to maximize sales.

Another of the real drivers behind this shift is the realization that without having separate sales and stock plans, there is no accountability by business units to make their sales plans. So if the first unit to allocate inventory gets the stock, then there may not be inventory for later drops of a catalog, e-mail campaigns, initial stocks to open stores, etc. Other companies use a "virtual inventory" concept, not in the sense of drop-shipping, but of the inventory system being able to keep planned sales by product and SKU by channel, and being able to reserve inventory for the channel business unit.

So if quantity of a product is 5,000 and 3,000 is for retail, 1,000 for Web and 1,000 for catalog, while the inventory is housed together in the same bulk and forward allocations, the inventory system keeps each channel's inventory protected. In this way business units are in control of their sales and stock performance.

Importing's effect

Where we source product is also changing how we can plan and manage it. Much of the multichannel world relies on imported product.

Even if you buy from a domestic distributor, chances are that merchandise is imported.

The initial markup, and hopefully the maintained gross margin, is significantly higher to offset the negatives that are cropping up in many businesses. The vendor minimums (often in thousands of pieces) are forcing companies to plan to use product in multiple seasons, leading to higher inventory investment and carrying costs. Long lead times (some below 13 weeks, but most 18-23 weeks) mean that purchase orders are placed long before the promotional planning is finalized, resulting in too much or insufficient stock. Using new products that are imports may lead to large overstocks if a product fails to sell as projected.

Additionally, companies may not be looking at a fully loaded product cost including agent's/broker's fees, demurrage, duty rate, product development costs, and buyer's travel. Couple that with warehouse storage space requirements for container size receipts and the inventory carrying costs. All of this leads to higher inventory and carrying costs and slower turnover.

What to do about it?

- Use mixed container loading, where appropriate.

- Weigh the increase in per unit cost to take smaller quantities.

- Move the entire merchandise and creative planning calendar for promotions back and do each season earlier (no easy task).

- Challenge merchants to look Stateside to try to get the product with smaller quantities, or to develop product in the U.S.

and later roll it out off-shore if it sells.

- Tackle the issue of accounting for all the product costs to be sure you have an accurate, fully loaded cost and sufficient initial markup without being overstocked.

Liquidating overstocks

Inventory that doesn't sell and liquidation are two dreaded aspects to merchandising. Because you have to take in larger imported orders and distribute to more channels, you need a cost effective strategy for in-season liquidation and clearance.

In a cost-based system it's hard to determine how much gross margin is lost in marking down retail prices. Our experience is that it may represent 2% to 4% of net sales at least.

What to do about it?

- Develop a liquidation strategy. Options include clearance catalogs, Web specials, bind-in or package inserts, sales pages, and telephone offers.

- Develop a report showing candidates for liquidation based on rate of sale.

- Develop an age of inventory report that will age products in time brackets (30 days, etc.) to stay on top of inventory.

Vendor compliance and supply chain

In most multichannel businesses the size of the product assortment and vendor base have grown dramatically. Supply chains have become increasingly complex with modes of transportation, importing, retail versus direct packaging, technology used in the supply chain and DCs, etc. All this necessitates setting standards with vendors so that you aren't working on an exception basis with every one.

Vendor compliance is at the heart of efficient supply chain management. Routing inbound shipments to reduce costs and scheduling inbound appointments can help speed product flow through the DC, significantly helping in turn to reduce inventory levels. Automating the supply chain through advanced shipping notifications (ASNs), RFID, and cross-docking to stores can go a long way toward reducing costs, but these cannot be implemented without a comprehensive vendor compliance policy.

Start small by communicating your company vision, the need for on-time delivery, routing guides, inbound dock standards like carton labeling, product specifications, accounting and paperwork requirements, contact list, and the costs of back orders. Begin a charge-back policy and implement it with your largest vendors. Later, you can add other items that are typically included, such as service level standards, packaging, labeling, case labeling, valued and value-added services, logistical requirements, scheduling appointments, cross-docking and direct-to-store requirements, charge back for non-compliance, etc.

The trend is to push compliance back up the supply chain. This means as many value-added services as possible — packaging, marking, quality inspections — performed by vendors or merchant reps in factories. Catching errors at the source and using source-based services speeds inventory flow, and any such issues are cheaper to deal with in the vendor's environment.

Organization overview

In larger retail specialty stores, merchandising is a separate organization from distributors or allocators who plan, manage and liquidate
inventory. Merchants select and source product. Distributors or allocators determine the quantity of product that goes to which stores, generally the quantity to purchase and reorder and when to take markdowns.

In department stores, buyers may still do the selection, vendor sourcing, and inventory control as a team divided into categories or departments. But larger retail businesses have adopted the distributor/
allocator model.

While the same group of merchants may select product for a multichannel business, store inventories and direct channels may be managed by separate inventory control groups.

Ten years ago, many companies had separate merchants for e-
commerce. Today, there are positions called Internet merchandising,
but they're more about how to depict product on the Website. Merchants and inventory control source, purchase, and manage most assortments.

In direct companies, inventory control is also split from merchandising (product selection and sourcing). The concept is that a separate
group will have more time to manage and analyze inventory and place
rebuys. Inventory control is where much of the everyday vendor communication on purchases, deliveries and compliance resides. The reality is that inventory control may be more attuned to working with advanced systems and analysis.

Many multichannel merchants today are hiring a forecaster rather than have each control buyer do the forecasting. An evolving business model has inventory control reviewing marketing's projections, getting their input and adjusting their projection systems to what they feel the plan is — if they feel that the catalog is faster or slower — to calculate more accurate inventory rebuy requirements.

Accountability for inventory

There are many inventory metrics that retail and multichannel businesses measure. Because the channels are different, the metrics vary. Here are a few of the major ones.

Retail: sales and stock plans; weeks of supply; store service levels (stock outs); turnover; gross margin return on investment (GMROI); returns; markdowns or write down plans; age of inventory; new store inventory coverage.

Catalog and e-commerce: sales and stock plans; turnover; gross margin return on investment (GMROI); cancellations; returns; markdowns or write downs; age of inventory; initial customer order fill rates; final order fill rates; coverage percentage when catalog mails.

The overall accountability of merchants, buyers and inventory managers for sales and inventory is important, since inventory is the largest single balance sheet asset, and how it's planned, managed and deployed largely determines customer service and profitability. Building some of the key measures into individual performance evaluations of buyers and inventory control personnel is essential.

This is old hat for large retailers, but direct marketers are implementing more metrics each year. Inventory management and its business models must evolve to meet multichannel growth.

How Nine Merchants Manage Distribution

	Business	Total Sales & % Direct	Total Assortment (Active SKUs Annually)	Shared DCs Between Channels?
Company A	Gen. merchant, 200+ stores	>$3 billion, 5% direct	>100,000	1 DC dedicated for direct; multiple retail DCs
Company B	Sporting goods, 50+ stores	>$2 billion, 25% direct	>100,000	3 DCs shared, all channels
Company C	Gen. merchant, 200+ stores	>$5 billion, 10% direct	>100,000	3 DCs dedicated to direct; multiple retail DCs
Company D	Women's apparel, 100+ stores	>$1 billion, 20% direct	25,000	1 DC dedicated to direct; 1 DC retail
Company E	Manufacturer, 50+ stores	>$1 billion, 20% direct	40,000 (apparel)	1 DC shared all channels
Company F	Specialty apparel, 100+ stores	>$1 billion, 15% direct	25,000	1 DC dedicated to direct; multiple retail DCs
Company G	Home and gifts, 50+ stores	>$750 million, 15% direct	25,000	1 DC shared all channels
Company H	Gifts and tabletop, 30 stores	>$100 million, 25% direct	10,000	1 DC shared all channels
Company I	Manufacturer, 50 stores	>$100 million, 15% direct	10,000 (women's and men's apparel)	1 DC shared for wholesale, retail, direct; some direct fulfillment from stores

Source: F. Curtis Barry & Company

As you can see from this chart of nine multichannel merchants, each with three or more channels, Companies B and C have three DCs across the country where direct orders are filled. Company C also fills store orders from the three DCs. Companies B and C are shortening the transportation time and cost to cover the entire country. But they have multiple DCs and staff, and have warehouse management and inventory systems that control order management for multiple facilities.

Why Importing Raises IRE

Most merchants couldn't stay in business without the margins that imported goods provide. But importing creates hardships in higher inventory and carrying costs. Imports also contribute to slower turnover, according to one vice president of inventory control for a large home decor merchant: "I don't have exact figures, but there is absolutely a relationship between increased importing and decreased turns. I know several other direct marketers who have experienced this," the VP says.

The decor marketer, which is about 40% imported, has also seen a significant increase of importing tax. What's more, "the past several years during peak spring receipts, we experienced backlogs at the receiving docks of several weeks," he adds. "The merchandise is especially bulky furniture and outdoor products, and very little could be done to flow goods in to prevent this." This cost the company thousands in surcharges for delays and backorders.

"It is often a difficult sell to the merchants, but I am a proponent of bringing a percentage of spring/summer merchandise in beginning January 1 to help alleviate some of the surge," the VP notes. Importing spring goods is often compounded by Chinese New Year (in late January or sometime in February), as many people in China take weeks off from work to prepare for and celebrate the holiday.

Importing heavily can certainly hit cash and backorder hard as well. When calculating/considering the retail price, merchants need to use a larger markdown percent for imported goods to accommodate for these extra expenses. "Five percent off the retail price is a good starting point," according to the VP.

Multichannel Merchandising 2.0
Developing A Cross-channel Merchandising Strategy

By Curt Barry

A company's merchandising strategy is at the heart of its growth and profitability. Saying that is not to minimize marketing and fulfillment's roles, but without strong merchandise you don't have a business. Great marketing cannot compensate for the lack of good product, though great marketing can radically improve the sales for product.

You can't look at merchandising in a vacuum. To be effective, merchandising has to go hand in glove with marketing in the retail, catalog, and e-commerce channels. Each channel has different strengths, and those in turn affect how well the channels sell merchandise.

As much as we hear these days about Web 2.0, leading multichannel merchants are taking their merchandising strategies to new and higher levels—a sort of multichannel merchandising 2.0—in which channels neither mirror nor compete with each other, but support each other in advancing company objectives.

Winning strategies today not only entail the consistency of look and feel between channels, but consistency of goals and of the retailer's ultimate objective: enhancing the customer's total experience. Achieving this customer-centric focus among all channels goes well beyond the old concepts of appearing seamless, and of merely showing the same products in multiple channels. It's more about how to gain synergy between the channels that should result in greater sales than if the channels operate separately.

Just how does merchandising tie into use by all channels? What are the best practices for merchandising retail, e-commerce, and catalog product—and how can multichannel merchants implement those practices?

Three-channel Excellence

The multichannel retailer that provides a consistent image in every sales channel makes it simpler for customers to find and buy what he offers. When customers know they can rely on a merchant to offer a positive experience in any channel, they are more likely to shop in any or all channels.

How well does one channel support the others? Consistency is provided in part by look and feel, as expressed by the company name, logo, mission statement, slogan, color schemes, label, shopping bags, gift wrap, and general design scheme—online, in the catalog, in stores. Synergy, however, cuts a lot deeper.

One of the retailers that does the best overall job of multichannel merchandising is Cabela's – The World's Foremost Outfitter© of hunting, fishing and outdoor gear (www.cabelas.com). When you consider their cross-channel expertise, it's impossible to separate the marketing and operational functions at which they excel.

In fiscal 2006, Cabela's earned $85.8 million on sales of $2.06 billion. Total revenue increased 14.7% from the previous year. Business from the direct cannels (catalog and e-commerce) increased 4.2% to $1.06 billion, primarily from e-commerce growth. Cabela's retail revenue increased 32.3% to $820.3 million, led by four new stores and a 1.3% increase in comparable store sales. Financial services increased 29.9% for the year through the Cabela's CLUB Visa credit card (Source: Cabela's letters to stockholders).

Even though Cabela's started as a cataloger, then migrated to e-commerce, with many of its stores ranging up to 250,000 sq.ft., it's rapidly becoming retail-driven. It's interesting to see a direct company successfully make this change to retail in a big way.

All three of Cabela's channels are massive and dominant in their merchandise niche. When shopping the stores, the product assortment looks to be several hundred thousand SKUs. The stores themselves are as near an outdoor experience as shopping can be. In the center of the stores is a multistory atrium called the Conservation Mountain with taxidermy mounts of various large game – elk, moose, bear, etc. – literally displayed on a mountain. Some stores we have been in have an African landscape. Others have a White Deer Museum which features record mounts and also abnormal antler configurations. Fish mounts ring the first floor of the store. Large freshwater aquariums show large regional species up close. I have seen elementary schools touring stores as if they were a natural history museum.

For Fall 2007 Cabela's produced a 1,392-page, hardbound catalog (weighing about 4 lbs. mailed in a box) for its best customers. Within a month or so, specialty catalogs such as *Waterfowl* (240 pages) and *Summer's Best Clothing and Footwear 2007* (128 pages) arrived in best customer's mailboxes. There are dozens of other specialized catalogs throughout the year.

The entire back cover of the master catalog is dedicated to the existing store locations—19 stores, and eight new stores scheduled for 2007. The cover shows small photo insets of stores. The Cabela's master catalog is a perfect example of cross-channel marketing and merchandising. It promotes the in-store and online Gun Library of world-class firearms and sporting collectibles, field test reports, and customer ratings and reviews, which are on the Web site. In addition the catalog offers comparison charts, buyers guides, and the online and in-store Bargain Cave ™ (10,000 products that are overstock, returns not restocked, special buys, and clearance items). Throughout the catalog, customers and employees are featured with their hunting and fishing trophies and testimonials about Cabela's products.

Cabela's produces the 60-minute television shows "Cabela's Outfitter Journal" and "Cabela's Memories in the Field". For "Memories in the Field", Cabela's asks viewers to send in their home videos of hunting and fishing adventures. If their videos are selected to be used, they receive $100 gift certificate to Cabela's. Cabela's also publishes the bimonthly *Outfitter Journal* magazine with in-depth articles from the most trusted and respected outdoor writers.

Clearly Cabela's has developed an high level of constant interplay between events and sales that are happening at its stores and on the Web site, and between marketing and merchandising as well.

The main point to be made here is that Cabela's in many ways makes it hard to separate one channel from another. For this multichannel merchant, maintaining synergy between the three channels is more important than looking at each channel as an isolated part of the business.

In other words, where merchandising and marketing are working in concert the total sales will be higher than if channels work independently of each other. In spite of this, some multichannel businesses still suffer from a fear of channel cannibalism, and allow different channels to compete with each other rather than concentrate on serving the customer. In fact, there are many multichannel retailers whose neglect of potential cross-channel synergy and consistency and end up with a Web site, retail stores, and catalog that appear to be separate businesses.

E-commerce edge

In multichannel commerce, e-commerce provides many options which retailers did not have before the advent of online sales.

Heather Dougherty, an analyst for Nielsen/Net Ratings (NTRT), states that JC Penney has one of the most productive Web sites among mainstream retailers. Nielsen/Net Ratings has consistently rated JC Penney's Web site among the top five Web sites nationally, based on the number of paying customers who visit the site.

Compared to Cabela's, JC Penney takes more of a traditional department store approach to multichannel retail. Anyone who looked at just Penney's catalog numbers, might reasonably conclude that the businesses have stalled, but looking at all channels, you see that business as a whole is really growing. In fact Penney's catalog sales have declined dramatically, but the company's overall/total sales are much better than they have been.

An interview with Bernie Feiwus, senior vice president of Penney Direct, suggests some of the reasons for the company's success. The Web site offers almost three times the number of products that are offered in Penney's retail stores. This gives the company a cost-effective way to sell bigger-ticket, often slower-turning items. Numbers from the company's financial reports also attest to the Web site's success. The company rang up over $1 billion in online sales in 2005, and sales through this channel are expected to overtake catalog sales, which declined from over $4 billion in the late 1990s to $1.7 billion last year.

The company has supported this growth in several creative ways. In August of last year, Penney began making Internet access available at 35,000 checkout registers. The retailer not only uses the Web as way to drive traffic to its retail stores, but encourages cooperation through channels with such initiatives. Penney was one of the first major retailers to allow its online customers to exchange and/or return items at its stores. [Sources: *Business Week*, "JC Penney Gets the Net," May 7, 2007; *DM News*, "JCP.com is the lynchpin in JC Penney's multichannel strategy," July 27,2007]

This sort of online support strategy can work in several ways. In tabletop businesses, for instance, e-commerce can create an advantage. Suppose that on average, only one in five customers want serving dishes and other accessories for a dinnerware set sold in a store. The store can avoid having to stock such slow-turning items in the stores by directing interested customers to its online store to view the complete dinnerware set.

Many channels, one strategy

In order to be sure that customers have a consistent experience across channels, the merchant has to put in place a multitude of policies and make them work with appropriate technology and training. For instance, customers should be able to expect the same level of customer service across channels. Customer service definitely includes the chance for a customer to talk to a live person or chat about a problem without spending hours looking online for a buried customer service number and then waiting for one of the small customer service staff to answer.

Industry professionals agree that improved technology and the increasing prevalence of online shopping in the last few years mean that more customers are conditioned to expect that their orders will ship the same day they're ordered, which would have been unheard of ten years ago. Multichannel merchants should offer seamless purchase and delivery options whether customers shop retail, catalog, online, or chose to pick it up in a store. Catalog and online orders should be available via quick shipment and at a reasonable shipping cost. That kind of channel inventory flexibility requires a willingness to ship (or allow customer pick up) from different channels to make the sale and satisfy the customer. Some direct businesses are gaining significant sales with drop-shipped product. One major retailer with direct sales over $200 million has 20% of its sales in drop ship. Similarly, there may be vendor assortments to which you can refer on your e-commerce site that do not take space in the catalog or store.

The company should accept gift cards/certificates as payment and be able to validate them online across channels. Returns and customer loyalty programs should operate across channels, and make pricing consistent across channels. In cases where prices actually need to be different, the merchant should have a standard policy to explain and handle such cases.

When developing your multichannel merchandising strategy, don't forget the importance of capturing a high percentage of data from all retail customer purchases and combining that with data from the direct channels. Many companies have found that multichannel customers achieve five to 10 times the value of single-channel customers. Mining the database allows businesses to know more about future merchandising by answering the question "What do the better customers buy, and what will keep them buying?"

Multichannel businesses can face serious conflicts between the structure of their merchandising organization and sales and performance goals that sacrifice customer satisfaction to meeting the goals. For example, when a company separates merchants by channel, it must deal with the issue of who controls inventory. In the early days of e-commerce, companies frequently hired a Web master who handled all aspects of online sales. Now, organizations have migrated from just trying to put product up online to having merchants who are responsible for what is shown and for the copy itself. More catalogers are hiring dedicated online merchandise managers (with varying authority) – somewhere between being a merchant with a plan to being the liaison between merchandising and Web master.

In many two-channel direct businesses, the online unit typically has a copywriter, a marketer or two, at least one merchandiser, a producer, and a tech team. Control of buying and inventory remains with merchandising and inventory control.

An organization that actively supports cross-channel merchandising should serve the customer without taking away accountability for channel managers, while at the same time maintaining a consistent merchandising direction. As businesses often make consolidated channel-buying decisions, not speaking with one voice to vendors, this can be a convoluted process.

Inventory management, purchasing, and open to buy functions can also present serious issues. Without inventory and order management systems that are integrated across channels, a business has limited visibility and will have difficulty shipping from stores, if that's a goal. Without real-time online inventory integration, it's impossible to know positively that you can ship for Web orders. An inability to move inventory or ship it from other channels to make the sale means inventory is frozen in one channel when it's needed in another. A multichannel solution requires the merchant to aggregate or roll up inventory quantities needed in a specified time frame in order to place POs and plan receipts.

Implementing the strategy

How do operations, finance, and systems match this synergistic approach? The majority of multichannel businesses still have fragmented systems. Lacking systems integration, they must maintain information in multiple channels, which means greater potential for errors and inconsistency between systems. The best way to achieve the goal of cross-channel consistency is to have single operational data stores and data warehouses across all channels for access to cross-channel product assortment. In other words, you'd like everybody to be using the same data – information entered into one system of record and moved electronically to multichannel systems.

The prescription to meet these needs starts with systems development. Open standards and service-oriented architecture (SOA), a way of designing programs so systems are integrated and can exchange data, is becoming more commonplace. More specifically, the sort of information needed to provide consistent customer experience and service across channels should include:

- Online, real-time visibility of inventory across channels
- Item master and pricing – products get priced via the item master, which has dozens of data points (description of item, vendor, when available, cost, retail selling price). Not having a single product master means a separate file or data base for each channel, greatly increasing the potential for error and inconsistency.
- Single vendor master
- Single purchase order writing and maintenance process
- Gift cards/certificates accepted as payment and validated online across channels
- Investigate alternative methods such as PayPal and Bill Me Later to gain more sales

- Returns accepted to any channel

- Overstock reduction and liquidation through stores and e-commerce. Determine what strategy gets the highest percentage of recovered cost.

- Customer loyalty programs across channels

- Consistent pricing and promotions across channels. This doesn't mean that better customers don't get specials or services (free shipping). It doesn't mean that there store sales or regional price points aren't sometimes necessary, but there must be a rationale for discrepancies, and that means a sophisticated product-pricing engine that can manage all channels. There might be regional competitive reasons to change prices. Major software vendors are still working on this.

- Ability to offer customized or special merchandising products

- Product copy and length may vary between channels, but there should be a single statement of product information of the particulars about the product that remains constant across channels.

- Investigate and experiment with Web 2.0 features that can sell more product—these include 360-degree views, online instructional and demo videos, zoom features, product reviews, community chat rooms, YouTube.com, etc.

- Improved search tools on Web. Implement improved Search Engine Optimization (SEO) to get your site highly ranked.

- What internal Web site search have you developed to make your site easier to find products and suggested purchases?

- Test new products on the Web and then roll them out.

Smaller and emerging companies

We've talked about the big companies. In reviewing smaller company strategies, here are some pointers more appropriate for smaller companies:

- Build the strongest e-commerce site that you can afford. Many smaller companies use package shopping carts or vendor front ends. Does this give your Internet business the sophistication it needs to compete?

- Do your catalog and e-commerce tie together with your stores in terms of "look and feel"?

- How are you achieving the synergy building sales between channels?

- How can you get more sales by extending vendor lines through e-commerce?

- Investigate and implement the operational aspects of making the customer experience consistent between channels.

In summary, along with the advance of e-commerce, multichannel merchandising has entered a new realm. Different channels of the same business no longer have to compete for sales. Encouraging creativity between marketing, merchandising, and retail management will make different channels more synergistic, increasing sales beyond what channels can do single-handedly.

Keeping Vendors Compliant
A Formal Compliance Program Can Help Reduce Costs

By Curt Barry

How important is vendor compliance? Imagine the following scenario: An apparel retailer's shipment of dresses for a catalog drop arrives late; in the meantime, hundreds of customer orders have gone on back order. Or how about this one: A hardware merchant finds that a shipment of tools has reached the distribution center — but the products are all the wrong sizes, because the factory failed to label them correctly.

These are the sorts of issues that vendor compliance policies seek to eliminate. Although it cannot eliminate every possible problem, a well-thought-out formal policy can protect you by specifying sanctions and charge-backs for vendors' mistakes.

While picking, packing, and shipping are the final steps in making sure customers get what they ordered, a truly efficient direct merchant will have planned to eliminate as many potential pitfalls as possible long before the merchandise is pulled off the shelf in the DC. At any significant scale of operation, the relationship between merchant and vendor has to run on more-structured and stringent guidelines than mutual trust. Companies without vendor compliance policies run a much greater risk of snafus than those that have spent the time it takes to develop detailed guidelines.

The Challenge

There's no doubt that rationalizing vendor relations poses a significant challenge to the retailer. All direct marketers receive goods from off-shore and/or domestic vendors. Most merchants have to handle in-bound consolidation of product from multiple vendors; multichannel merchants may need to cross-dock shipments directly to stores with-out opening, inspecting, or repackaging them. All merchants use re-verse logistics to consolidate their inevitable returns, and many may also be faced with such complex, vendor-related logistics as ware-house-to-warehouse transfers, vendor-direct-to-store shipments, or merchandise shipped from a vendor to the closest warehouse that then must be allocated to other warehouses.

So it's easy to see why vendor compliance is at the heart of efficient supply chain management. Routing inbound shipments to reduce costs and scheduling inbound appointments can help speed product flow through the DC, significantly helping in turn to reduce inventory lev-els. Automating the supply chain through advanced shipping notifica-tions (ASNs), RFID, and cross-docking to stores can go a long way to reducing costs, but these measures are not a substitute for a compre-hensive vendor compliance policy.

Considering that labor accounts for 50% of the cost per order, any-thing a merchant can do to reduce the number of times product is touched — by way of repackaging, marking, and inspection, for in-stance — will help to reduce those costs. Domestic inbound freight accounts for 2%-4% of the cost of goods sold. Although offshore sourcing costs are higher, the increased margin pays for freight and product development costs. Some industries are especially prone to high labor costs. Because of the high return rates in the apparel indus-try, for example, costs for receiving and returns can be as much as 30%-35% of a DC's total direct labor costs.

All Aboard

Establishing and monitoring vendor compliance is a team effort among the merchandising, operations, finance, and inventory control departments. Everyone has to be in agreement. In fact, a frequent obstacle to implementing vendor compliance programs is that merchants are afraid that a more comprehensive and careful accounting may upset vendor relationships that they have worked to develop. The merchant has to weigh that possibility against the probability that improved vendor compliance will reduce costs and improve customer service over time.

For the many companies that have major problems in processing receipts in a timely fashion — those companies that incur higher warehouse costs and costs per order than their competitors, and whose store replenishments are not streamlined to flow through their DCs to stores or directly to stores from vendors — vendor compliance is a necessary step to reducing costs by increasing efficiency.

Without a formal vendor compliance policy, the warehouse has no recourse but to absorb both direct and hidden costs for noncompliance. Without compliance it is impossible for a merchant to implement advanced supply chain systems, ASNs, just-in-time inventory, source marking and ticketing, or future RFID programs. A good vendor compliance policy will not only avoid pitfalls, but it also will help the merchant get receipts on time and in compliance, which in turn will reduce the time spent dealing with vendor disputes, claims, and charge-backs.

Making it Formal

Ultimately vendor compliance works best when a company can clearly state to its vendors consistent compliance parameters and goals

— and just as important, specific sanctions for noncompliance. The major benefits of a formal vendor compliance policy are significant: reduced cost of warehousing, reduced freight in, and increased speed of processing orders and through-to-store replenishments. These benefits in turn have a direct effect on customer satisfaction because they reduce return rates due to incorrect sizing, color, and damages.

How comprehensive should a vendor compliance policy be? Best practice calls for a company to develop a detailed, written policy and to then enforce it by instituting a charge-back policy to which both vendors and management agree. In general, a merchant should aim to push compliance back up the supply chain. One way to accomplish this is to have as many value-added services as possible — packaging, marking, quality inspections — performed by vendors or merchant reps in factories. Catching errors at the source and using source-based services speeds inventory flow, and any such issues are cheaper to deal with in the vendor's environment.

It's a good idea to ask the vendors to review the policy, sign off on it, and fax the signed copy back to inventory control. Many multichannel companies also have their compliance policy manuals on their Website and give vendors a link to it.

Starting a program may seem daunting, since a fully developed vendor compliance manual for a midsize company can run to 50 single-spaced pages of instructions and explanations. Such manuals have usually been developed over time, and although the draft of a new manual may be based on an example from another business, each individual company will have to use its own history and data to develop a compliance manual.

If you're just beginning to implement a comprehensive vendor compliance policy, it may be more useful to concentrate on some areas over others. Here are some key compliance starting points:

- Create a routing guide (or shipping instructions) that tells vendors how to ship small packages, pallets, and containers via the carriers you have negotiated rates with. The shipping instructions should include when to use which transportation companies based on weight, dimensions, and other criteria. Vendors charge a 20%-60% premium for shipping, so a best practice that yields big savings is to switch from vendor-paid to collect or third-party consignee billing.

- Make human-readable and bar-code labeling requirements.

- On-time merchandise delivery should be a priority.

- Enforce quality by stating item specifications for each product.

Charge-back rates vary widely, and it's up to the individual merchant to determine the real charge-back costs in his business. On the low end of the scale charges are $25-$50 per shipment, but some companies charge $100 or more per shipment (see "What can go wrong: vendor charge-back categories" table). For late shipment of merchandise that causes backorders, companies use a cost per backorder — $7-$12 in actual cost for most companies. Or they may use a graduated percent of the cost value of the late shipment and invoice.

Success Stories

Here are several examples of what retailers have saved by developing, adopting, and enforcing vendor compliance policies:

- Scuba gear merchant Divers Direct — with eight stores, a catalog, and a Website — achieved a gross margin improvement of

0.7% and better accounting control. With Federal Express consignee billing, its vendors now use FedEx as the preferred carrier, so Divers Direct can better manage its inbound shipments and realize significant savings on inbound freight costs. Another benefit is to use FedEx InSight to track shipments online and then to use FedEx DirectLink to download invoices automatically and allocate all freight invoices to the appropriate general ledger accounts.

- Timberland, which sells footwear, apparel, and accessories, improved its inbound visibility using a "scan and pack" process as product was packed at factories in Asia (90% of Timberland's product is imported). Shipment-related data, including container number and packing list, are sent electronically to the retailer's receiving system.

- In October 2005, Wal-Mart touted the early results of its mandated RFID compliance program. They are impressive: It has reduced out-of-stocks by 16% in stores where RFID is installed, as well as reduced excess inventory. It is three times faster to restock RFID-tagged items than to restock comparable items that are instead marked with bar codes. Overall, RFID-enabled stores were 63% more effective in replenishing out-of-stocks than the control stores.

As automation helps extend supply chains, the last frontier in efficiency and in automation may well be the way in which direct merchants manage their vendor relations. Those that ignore this potentially volatile aspect of their operations do so at their peril, while those with a seasoned, well-planned vendor compliance program can achieve significant savings.

Look it Up in the Manual

Vendor compliance manuals typically address these elements:
- Company history, vision, and expectations for customers
- Cost of backorders to the business
- Service standards
- On-time delivery to committed delivery date
- Products delivered in proper condition, delivered in agreed upon manner
- Product quality according to specs
- Product packaging and polybag specs
- Label marking for retail shipments vs. direct
- Supply chain systems requirement (electronic POs, ASNs, etc.)
- Master pack and inner pack sizes
- Case labeling guidelines
- Accounting and paperwork requirements
- Logistical requirements
- Routing guides to reduce costs
- Scheduling appointments
- Cross-docking requirements
- Direct-to-store requirements
- Drop-ship instructions
- Schedule of charge-backs for noncompliance
- Customer return of merchandise and credits
- Contact list, including merchandising, distribution center, accounts payable, drop- ship orders, and inventory control

What Can Go Wrong: Vendor Charge-Back Categories

The following is a sample of chargeback categories from a midsize direct merchant whose vendor compliance manual is 25 pages long:

- Improper purchase order (PO) number on carton or label
- Wrong product sent
- Product not labeled with SKU #
- Style or product substitution without approval
- Inbound receipt past cancellation date
- Incorrect labels or placement of labels
- Merchandise not bagged to specs
- Product not labeled with country of origin
- Shipment lacks certificate of origin
- Invalid PO
- Product specs not sent in advance of shipment
- No photo sample
- Merchandise not packaged according to specs, repackaging required
- Early shipment without approval
- Merchandise required 100% inspection
- Mixed POs on pallet or in cartons
- Mixed SKUs per carton
- Failure to meet cross-dock-to-store requirements
- Bill of lading not complete
- Shipment did not conform to routing guide
- Late delivery, causing backorders
- Merchandise damage not attributed to carrier
- Did not ship in correct option
- Incorrect placement of packing list, incomplete packing list, no packing list
- Shipment on nonstandard pallet
- Failure to protect fragile merchandise
- Delivery to wrong address
- Delivery without appointment

The Best Of Inventory
Fourteen best practices for managing your merchandise

By Curt Barry

Inventory management and forecasting are strategic issues. Companies that recognize this fact can typically provide higher levels of service to their customers and post higher profits.

Developing a comprehensive inventory strategy involves a number of departments — including fulfillment, marketing, and merchandising — as well as inventory control. It also involves implementing inventory best practices. Here are 14 best practices that will most likely benefit your business the most.

1. **Synchronize promotions**

   Successful strategic inventory management relies on tying creative and marketing plans to merchandising plans. Marketers and merchants need to develop companywide planning calendars and projections for all promotions in all channels — catalog, online, e-mail, stores, space ads. Merchants and the inventory control group then plan product purchasing, availability, and receipts to support these events.

   There are three aspects to this planning. First, the marketing department compiles and continually updates the marketing calendar. Second, the marketing team plans the expected orders by week for the promotions. Third, the inventory control and merchandising teams plan the demand in units for the promotions.

Often it's e-mail campaigns that trip up multichannel merchants. The campaigns may appear on the marketing calendar, but all too frequently no one decides which items will be promoted until four to eight weeks before the actual date of the promotion. By then product has been ordered and may already have arrived in the distribution center. This lack of planning can cause contention between channels for best-sellers, leading to customer frustration and backorders.

2. **Revamp the organizational structure**
   To implement more-streamlined inventory practices, many companies have adopted a new organizational structure: The merchandising department handles product selection, sourcing, and development and works with the creative department on promotions. The inventory control group is primarily responsible for overseeing the prior season's category and item history, working with the merchants on assortment planning, managing the inventory, forecasting, reordering, receipt planning, post-mortem evaluation of item performance, and vendor communication and compliance. Merchandising may still place initial purchase orders, but in most cases inventory control will pick up relationships with vendors and do the necessary reordering and stock balancing.

3. **Take a longer view of item planning**
   Rather than planning items one promotion at a time, plan an item across promotions. Doing so enables you to plan receipts in line with promotions, reduce backorders, make minimum order requirements, and significantly reduce planning time.

4. **Enforce vendor compliance**
   The inventory control team is generally responsible for adminis-

trating vendor compliance policies because they communicate most frequently with the vendors. One of the basic goals of a compliance program is to push inspection up the supply chain. Problems can be more readily corrected if they are identified before product ships to the distribution center rather than upon arrival at the DC. Compliance policies should include routing guides, item specification sheets, retail and direct packaging, accounting and paperwork standards, company contact lists, chargeback policies and schedules, and advance shipment notice (ASN) and systems standards.

5. **Track key inventory metrics**
   An industrial engineering axiom states that what isn't measured can't be improved. From an inventory perspective, the metrics are the same for online sales as for catalogs, although the forecasting systems requirements for Internet promotions may be different from those for catalog inventory. The metrics include:

   A.top-line and bottom-line growth
   B.maintained gross margin
   C.initial customer order fill rate (see chart)
   D.final fill rate/returns/cancellations
   E.gross margin return on investment (GMROI)
   F.turnover
   G.cost of backorders
   H.age of inventory
   I.measures of overstock
   J.write-downs as a percentage of costs.

   Key metrics for stores would include:
   A.top-line and bottom-line growth
   B.comparable-store sales (year over year)

C.maintained gross margin

D.turnover

E.GMROI

F.weeks of supply

G.markdowns/margin loss from write-downs

H.age of inventory

I.sell-through percent

J.stock-to-sales ratios

6. **Select the right systems**

   At the heart of capturing these metrics are your retail and direct systems. Keep in mind that metrics produced by systems will be used for dashboard reporting to top management and that management will need drill-down capability to see details at lower levels of reporting such as merchandise divisions.

   Ideally a multichannel merchant wants to implement channel-appropriate merchandise planning, inventory forecasting, trending, and performance systems now. In the real world, many multichannel companies are still working through what their requirements are specifically for e-mail and Internet forecasting functions. Analyze your Internet demand and determine how different it is from catalog demand, and develop systems functions accordingly.

7. **Master the art of master scheduling**

   A system with master-scheduling capability takes into account all promotional plans by item. It will also add demand projections by week, subtract returns and cancellations, add in the expected receipts and plot delivery dates for purchase orders (Pos), and then calculate whether an item is running short or overstocked across channels. Because the calculations are by week, you can see where more on order is needed or the effect of delaying Pos on the net requirements.

To acquire a system with this capability, management needs to make a significant investment. In a recent client study the costs ranged from $400,000 to $1.5 million. Software companies are looking to develop full-fledged retail, Internet, and catalog planning and inventory management functionality; no one vendor has all the functions needed today.

8. **Adhere to exception reporting**
   A natural outgrowth of systems with master scheduling, exception reporting helps rebuyers and inventory managers know where to take action without their having to review every item every week in detail. Retail and direct inventory systems both use exception reporting. Types of exception reports include:

   A. management reports (for instance, top 50/bottom 50 in sales)
   B. product characteristic reports (e.g., all items in a certain fabric across departments)
   C. POs needed based on stock-out calculations, on hand and on order, and projected demand with item/vendor lead time
   D. ranking reports for returns, cancellations, gross margin, and liquidation
   E. forecast variance plan to actual
   F. slow sellers and candidates for liquidation
   G. new vs. repeat performance
   H. imported vs. domestic product.

9. **Identify lost demand**
   To capture and plan for phantom, or shadow, demand, catalogers must record order information in the contact center. For Web

sales, analytics systems are starting to have the capability to report when items move in and out of a customer's order process. Once you've captured the metrics, you need to report to the merchants the consequences of being out of stock in cases when customers substituted items for those that were sold out. Then the numbers need to get into merchandise planning for the next season. Catalogs have found that best-sellers that were out of stock might have been able to sell an additional 10%-30% based on phantom demand.

10. **Plan by assortment**

Preseason assortment planning of categories and products relies on the past sales performance of items or, for items not sold in the past, similar product, along with item availability. Retail assortment planning is top down by category and bottom up by item.

11. **Track inbound receipts**

Inbound tracking of receipts not only benefits the fulfillment operation but also helps inventory management. Smaller companies often lack this capability, and it can really hurt their DC planning and their customer service. But many freight consolidators and carriers, including United Parcel Service and FedEx, offer tracking services. Or you can implement inbound systems so that vendors send ASNs when purchase orders have shipped. UPS and FedEx both provide this service.

12. **Create coverage reports**

Coverage is defined as having sufficient quantities of products already in the DC when a promotion is in-home. Companies need to develop coverage reports to show how much is in DC vs. the initial demand projected. There are always some games played in this area with management. Because 50% or more of orders related to a catalog drop take place in the first four weeks after the drop, if you don't have sufficient quantities of a product by the time the catalogs hit mailboxes, you're going to create backorders early in the promotion.

Merchandising and inventory control need to follow up closely with vendors to ensure higher initial coverage by the time first orders arrive. As for the initial coverage rate, defined as the quantity of units in stock by product and SKU before a catalog mails or an e-mail promotion is sent, you should have sufficient coverage for the first two to three weeks in all SKUs, but most businesses are well below these levels.

13. Balance understock/overstock

What is the balance point between the cost of being out of stock on an item ($7-$12 per unit on backorder, according to our proprietary studies) and the cost of overstock (margin loss you experience from liquidating categories of product)? Chief financial officers often try to identify this at a top level. Merchants and inventory control experts need to identify how much risk lies in being under- or overstocked as they do the merchandise planning. New items, exclusives, and imports obviously have much more risk. Exclusives and imported merchandise may also have higher minimum quantities.

14. Optimize your SKUs

SKU optimization crosses finance, DC, and inventory lines. In the past decade, many catalogs expanded the range of color and size SKUs for individual items, and sales increased accordingly. Merchandise with high SKU counts (bedding, shoes, apparel) creates the biggest challenges. Now companies recognize that the cost of fulfillment (labor, space) and liquidation for slow-moving items can be high compared with their actual sales. SKU profitability or optimization needs to be determined with fully loaded costs (advertising costs, fulfillment costs, overhead, etc.

Best Practices in Inventory Management

Unless a company has a proprietary credit program, inventory will generally be its largest balance-sheet asset - and knowing standard inventory metrics is the key to protecting that asset. Here are some best-practice standards:

Initial Order Fill Rate

Customer orders shipped complete
Advanced fashion: 70%-80%
Reorderable, basic apparel: 80%-90%
Gifts/housewares: 85%-95%
Business products: 98%-100%

Final Order Fill Rate

Of the orders taken over the life of a catalog, the percentage of customer orders ultimately shipped 100% complete.
Advanced fashion: 90%-95%
Reorderable, basic apparel: 95%-99%
Gifts/housewares: 96%-100%
Business products: 100%

Return Rates

Percentage of gross demand that is returned by the customer regardless of the reason
Advanced fashion: 20%-40%
Reorderable, basic apparel: 10%-20%
Gift/housewares: 2%-4%
Business Products: 1%-3%

Cancellation Rate

The percentage of customer demand that is canceled by either the customer (from backorders) or the company (permanently out of stock)

Apparel: 2%-5%

Gifts/housewares: 2%-4%

Business products: 1%

Inventory Turnover Rate

The annual cost of goods sold divided by the average inventory, at cost

Apparel: 3-5

Gifts/housewares: 4-6

Business products: 6-8

Gross Margin Return on Investment (GMROI)

You'll need to know the turnover to measure your gross margin return on investment: maintained margin (decimal) x turnover = GMROI. Our studies indicate that good performance is over 2.00. To see how even small improvements in either gross margin or turnover can improve results, plug in your stats. Improve one or the other by a moderate amount and see how the GMROI improves.

Most Catalogs don't measure and report a weekly order fill rate; instead they only measure initial item fill rate or backorders. Initial order fill represents what percentage of the orders shipped complete (all items on an order) in the DC's order turnaround time standard. This is an excellent measure of customer service.

ABCs Of Effective Nonprofit Merchandising

Nonprofit organizations that rely on catalogs and other retail vehicles to boost donations and further their missions can take some lessons from the for-profit world.

By Curt Barry

How can a $20 lace nightgown help fight cancer? What good can a candle shaped like a moccasin be to a child whose family can't afford to send him to school?

These products, and thousands like them, appear in catalogs produced by nonprofit organizations to increase contributions and educate donors. The American Cancer Society sells the nightgown, along with accessories made with cancer patients in mind, in its "TLC" catalog; the shoe-shaped candle appears in the Southwest Indian Foundation's tome. No matter what the cause, nonprofits that sell products, either through a catalog or on the Internet, must run their contact centers and fulfillment operations efficiently and competitively in order to keep costs low and customer satisfaction high.

Focus on the product

Product is the single most important aspect of a profitable catalog business and is central to nonprofits using catalogs, retail stores and Internet sites. Increasing revenue per catalog is all about increasing the number of products, pages and page density.

"Product development is one of my major concentrations," says Liz Grainer, executive director for retail marketing at The Art Institute of Chicago. "How products in the retail stores, catalog and on the Internet site relate to the institute's collection and mission is a key to success. The Institute in the past five years has moved from having 60 percent of the product being open-market vendor merchandise to 60 percent proprietary-developed product unique to the institute. The products relate to the Institute's collection, different cultures and exhibitions in progress."

Exclusive and proprietary product differentiates product-selling nonprofits from other catalogs and retail stores and helps organizations achieve considerably higher gross margins. Hard-goods and gift catalogs need to have a gross demand of $2 per catalog mailed to make money. Apparel typically increases gross demand but suffers from high return and cancellation rates. Overall, apparel catalogs generally exceed $2 revenue per catalog.

Bill McCarthy, executive director of the Southwest Indian Foundation, has mastered the development of high-quality Indian jewelry, pottery, kachina dolls and other Native American-related gifts, books, music, clothing and videos. The catalog entity has created jobs for Indian artisans of the Navajo tribe and the pueblo tribes of the Zuni, Laguna, Acoma and Hopi. Since 1990, McCarthy has increased SWIF's proprietary items from 10 products pictured on one page, which was folded and inserted into a No. 10 envelope, to the 375 products in the 120-page catalog for spring, which will have a circulation of 14 million.

To make the best use of space in a catalog, there are some basic rules of thumb to consider. First, assuming that new products are equal in mail-order buyer appeal to existing products, demand will increase anywhere from 25 percent to 50 percent of the corresponding space-

smith, cabinetmaker, etc. will be offered online."

No matter what the cause, it pays for nonprofits to train contact center and fulfillment staffs to answer questions about their missions and the people/causes they serve. Sales representatives at the National Wild-life Federation are trained not only to sell but also to answer questions about clean water, wolf populations, backyard bird and animal habi-tats, and a host of other NWF issues, according to Carole Fox, vice president of operations at NWF. Scientific or highly technical calls are referred to the pros.

Key financial elements

In order to make money, nonprofit catalogs, like their consumer-based cousins, must manage seven financial areas. For-profit catalogs typi-cally earn 5 percent to 10 percent or higher of the net sales after all expenses. While there might be dozens of line items on a profit-and-loss statement, managing for profitability comes down to controlling these seven critical elements:

Gross margin. Catalogs typically earn a gross margin that is in a range of 52 percent to 58 percent. In recent years, many organizations have dramatically in-creased the percent of imported products their catalogs carry, which has improved the initial markup.

Advertising costs. This is the total cost of creating, printing and mail-ing the catalog. As a percentage of net sales, it typically ranges from 25 percent to 35 percent. Admittedly, catalogs are an expensive adver-tising tool. But when well-merchandised offerings are sent to targeted mail-order buyer lists, they are the most productive way to sell prod-uct.

There are fixed and variable components to the advertising costs. The fixed cost to create a page includes the design, copy, models, photography, film, color separations, etc. Catalogs using in-house creative typically range from $1,300 to $1,900 per page, and catalogs using a creative agency can range from $2,000 to $3,500 per page. Many catalogs use a combination of in-house and freelance creative, adding up to costs of $1,800 to $2,200 per page. The variable costs, which include printing, paper, the assembly and binding process, list rentals, and postage, etc., are per-copy costs and vary depending on how many copies you print and mail.

Contact center and fulfillment. Consulting firm F. Curtis Barry & Co.'s proprietary benchmarking studies of catalog companies have shown that the most cost-effective contact center and fulfillment costs are typically 8 percent to 15 percent of net sales. For smaller entities, it's important - and often difficult - to get costs under 20 percent of net sales.

Net sales comparisons can vary widely based on average order. From a cost-per-order perspective, efficient companies average $8-$13 for fully loaded costs.

Front-end costs. Efficient order processing costs $4-$6 for data-entry and contact center operations, including direct and indirect labor, benefits, credit processing, occupancy and telecom costs.

Back-end costs. Efficient order processing costs $4-$7 for merchandise processing and fulfillment, including direct and indirect labor, benefits, occupancy and shipping materials. It does not include outbound shipping costs or an offset with shipping and handling revenue that varies widely between catalogs. When these are taken into account, they distort the picture of the cost of fulfillment between catalogs.

General costs. These are the costs of buying, marketing, accounting, human resources and IT that are part of the business unit. Typically, in profitable catalogs, G&A costs are 9 percent to 11 percent.

Returns and cancellations. Everyone knows that sales are what gets booked in accounting and deposited in the bank. But demand - orders in the door - is very important. There are two ways that demand gets eroded to yield lower net sales: cancellations and returns. Customer cancellations because of back orders are ideally 2 percent or less. For hard goods, this is often achievable. For apparel and soft goods that have a higher fashion design and more new products that are difficult to forecast, the average may be more typically 3 percent to 4 percent. When bestsellers strip the inventory, cancellations can range into high single digits.

The natural return rate for hard goods, home decor and jewelry can range from less than 2 percent to 9 percent depending on the category. Apparel, which achieves a much higher revenue per catalog, also has a much higher return rate of 10 percent to 15 percent. Add in shoes or other products with a more tailored, size-oriented or multiple-color SKU base - and high-fashion apparel has an even higher return rate of 20 percent to 35 percent.

In conclusion

Non-profits have made good use of catalogs and fulfillment for fund development, donor solicitation and mission advancement. But merchandising and mailing catalogs means that you have to run the operation by the rules and metrics of businesses in the for-profit world.

Multichannel Inventory:
What You Need To Know

By Curt Barry

It sounds like a sci-fi trilogy: Past, present, and future merge to provide a single, optimal inventory experience. Multichannel merchants manage inventory seamlessly throughout major business processes and across channels in order to find the perfect balance between customer service and profitability.

Few merchants today would claim to have reached this level of inventory management, as developing such a strategy can be complex. But there are compelling economic reasons to try.

In most multichannel companies, inventory is the largest dollar asset on the balance sheet, which means that how well you plan, forecast, and manage inventory will to a large degree determine your profitability. Inaccurate forecasting ultimately produces backorders, and backorders can result in dissatisfied current customers; they can also turn away potential new customers.

Although the cost of poor inventory management doesn't have a separate line on a company's P&L statement, it can be steep. According to our proprietary studies with dozens of companies, the true cost of a backordered unit of merchandise runs from $7 to $12. For a company processing 200,000 orders a year, with an average of two items per order and a 20% backorder rate, the operations cost to the company could run as high as $480,000. This does not include costs related to prospecting, expediting backorders by inventory control, returns because of late shipments, lost margin, additional air freight, and customer ill will or losing the customer all together.

Faulty planning and forecasting can also produce overstocks that must be liquidated, at a loss of as much as 4%-10% of merchandise margin (between initial purchase margin and maintained margin), depending on the product category.

Direct marketers are well aware that they need to resolve inventory issues across channels. In a recent AMR Research survey of retailers' plans for upgrading their multichannel systems, 22% of the respondents cited Web-enabled inventory management system and visibility as a key strategy they will be working on in the next 12 months. The AMR report, "Technology Trends in Inventory for Retailers and CP Manufacturers," went on to say, "The lack of data consolidation for inventory and order management further illustrates retailers' immature inventory management and order processes." The report also lists customer loyalty and multichannel customer order fulfillment among the top five concerns of respondents.

Creating a Strategy

Few would argue with the benefits of a multichannel inventory strategy, but many may struggle with creating such a program. We've identified a few steps to begin the process.

Start by analyzing key inventory metrics and P&L figures regarding inventory performance and customer service in your company. These include initial and final order fill rates, initial and final item fill rates, cancellations and returns as an erosion of gross demand, markdowns and liquidations, gross margin, and reduction of inbound freight costs and its effect on cost of goods sold. The chart "Key merchandise metrics for direct marketers" compares some important statistics for various categories.

You should then compare your company's results to statistics that describe good inventory performance in similar types of businesses. If you are a high-end fashion retailer, for instance, metrics for an online gift business won't be of much use in comparisons. The kind of statistical information you need is not easily available, however. To gain this knowledge you may need to hire a consultant, exchange information with other businesses, or join inventory benchmarking Share-Groups.

Next, review processes to determine where improvement can occur. Where are the problem areas? Your assessment should pay special attention to these issues:

- How in sync are marketing events and media and merchandise plans? From a merchandising perspective, are the demand and receipt plans in line with marketing's weekly projections?
- Is there comprehensive product and campaign history with which to plan new promotions? If not, are you capturing history for a future planning system?
- How effective is the preseason and event merchandise planning?
- How accurate is the daily and weekly forecasting for the channels?
- Does your company have a comprehensive postseason analysis for items and promotions that merchandising can use in planning the new season?
- Do your existing systems help rebuyers to stay on top of fast sellers, write purchase orders, come up with candidates for liquidation, and follow through with vendors? Or must rebuyers wade through mountains of data to find where to take action?

- Are there backup and cancelable purchase orders with vendors to correct for errors and omissions during the initial merchandise planning and the current rate of sale?
- Do you have cost-effective methods in place to liquidate over-stocks?

After completing this part of the analysis, you'll need to develop a list of options and solutions for improvement. Prioritize them based on benefits. Assess the risks associated with the plan as well as any gains you expect to achieve. You must also determine what these improvements will cost and then include the costs of systems to be developed or acquired, the organizational changes needed to implement the plan, and any additional inventory.

At a management level, agree on a plan to implement and change business practices. You need to determine how this plan will improve inventory performance and customer service.

Integrated Planning and Forecasting

For inventory purposes, it's important that e-mail and Internet promotions are a part of a total media/circulation plan that also encompasses catalog drops and in-store promotions. Only a few years ago, when Internet sales commonly represented no more than 10% of total sales for multichannel companies, the merchants would simply increase the overall buying plan by that percentage to account for the new channel. Now that online sales often account for up to 40% of a company's total sales, merchants must figure out how demand for individual items varies in each channel. You can accomplish this by performing a category/item analysis for each channel.

To integrate marketing and merchandising plans, start by developing a companywide calendar for all channels, which should include store promotions, catalog merchandise drops, e-mail blasts, display ads, and so on. In turn, merchandise planning by the merchants and inventory management for each channel must key off this integrated schedule. Integration of channels in terms of inventory planning is basically about preseason and in-season forecasting once the promotion is active.

Analysts today have access to quantitative forecasting and purchase-planning systems and numerical analysis approaches to historical data by season, item, and catalog or promotion. As a result, forecast accuracy has continued to improve. But to a large degree, given the nature of merchandising and customer preferences, effective inventory forecasting still must rely on the intuitive experience and cooperation of merchandising, marketing, and creative.

All the complexities of cooperation, intuition, and analysis that go into the forecasting process are part of a continuous cycle through the life of the promotion. Every new catalog or promotion begins a forecasting lifecycle, and the information determined in each phase of merchandise planning and analysis must be reconciled with other planning levels and with the overall business plan.

To improve overall forecasting accuracy and in-stock position, the marketing department should forecast demand weekly (if not daily for online sales) to create a detailed baseline. While merchandising may not be able to react via reordering or expediting stock each week — let alone every day — the department needs to be informed so that they can make decisions for purchase and receipt planning.

But the major planning issue for multichannel merchants continues to be the integration of plans and forecasts by product/SKU from all channels, beginning with seasonal planning and proceeding with in-season or active forecasting once a promotion is live.

The Best-Laid Plans

A multichannel inventory plan with the wrong infrastructure will face as many difficulties as an organization without a plan. Here are some of the organizational decisions required to implement a strategic plan successfully:

1. Separate buying responsibilities from inventory management

Best practice in many mature multichannel businesses is to separate the buying and inventory management functions. The merchants or the buyers focus on what the customer wants, product knowledge and styles, developing exclusives, product specifications and design, where to source merchandise, and negotiating the initial vendor purchase. In line with making the process strategic, the inventory management system takes charge of demand analysis, forecasting, merchandise planning, purchasing and re-buying, maintaining the vendor relationship, maintaining compliance standards, working with the vendors to get merchandise in on time, maintaining proper inventory levels, and postseason and campaign analysis. This division of labor gives the buyers more crucial time to source product; it also puts more personnel in place to improve planning, forecasting, and analysis.

2. Plan and analyze inventory across channels

Put in place individuals who can perform planning and analysis across channels, consolidating inventory data to a single set of buying and liquidation actions while combining inventory requirements across channels. Since individual channels often use specialized systems, the challenge is to interpret the selling trends properly and to come up with a single set of requirements for product to be purchased in the proper time frame.

3. Maintain channel inventory flexibility

When stocks are low, make decisions about which channel can best serve the customer, and free up available stock for that channel, on a day-to-day basis. Plan how these decisions will be made and who will make them.

4. Assign responsibility for liquidation of overstocks

Empower an inventory manager or a merchant to manage liquidation media aggressively. To a large degree, the characteristics of your merchandise — the percentage of new products, exclusives, and imported items — determine your merchandise strategy. New products, being without history, are extremely difficult to forecast and can result in the greatest number of overstocks or backorders. The only reasonable approach to help the merchant reach a decision about the quantity of new product he might sell is to compare a new item with a similar product that has a selling history.

Even then, the range of error can exceed 40%. In such cases, historical sales figures of similar items and categories over an entire promotion period during a similar season are at best a gauge. On the other hand, runaway best-sellers can strip inventories, generate backorders, and destroy profitability by driving up backorder costs.

Products with long lead times — those sourced offshore, private-label products, items that require fabric design or component parts — call for a commitment to an inventory level long before any marketing decisions are made, sometimes 8-10 months in advance of a promotion. This means reorders, if you can get them, will be of large volumes and long lead times (six to eight weeks).

Strong Vendor Relationships

Planning and forecasting is an inexact science. One of the most effective strategies for achieving a high initial fill rate without overstocks is to develop and maintain good relationships with your major vendors. Merchants and vendors must develop a plan to provide backup stocks and cancelable purchase orders whenever possible. Optimal inventory requires products from vendors who can meet specific criteria on time and also supply sudden, unexpected demand.

Good vendor relationships require your company to take a proactive role with vendors, communicating with them weekly through the first few weeks of a promotion. Strong vendor relationships may rely on tools such as electronic data interchange (EDI) or Web-based information exchange systems. Vendors need to know total plans for a given item as well as timing for receipt of merchandise in relation to the overall marketing strategy. For catalogs it takes two weeks of selling (roughly 20% of orders, for instance) and three weeks on color/size SKUs to forecast needs accurately based on percentage-complete projections. Internet curves are generally shorter.

The participation and support of top management is essential to achieving better vendor relationships without stepping on the toes of merchandisers. Tightening vendor relations almost always involves difficult decisions, however. It may mean reducing the total number of vendors in order to increase the merchant's impact with a smaller number. It may involve extensive vendor education and negotiating penalty and payback fees for vendor mistakes.

The best way to work with vendors is to implement a proactive, planned buying strategy based on these tactics:

- As purchase orders are written, negotiate back-up stock and planned cancelable purchase orders for an item.

- Develop a coverage report broken about by SKU and by stock on hand. Get the inventory managers to follow up with all vendors several weeks in advance of the promotion in order to avoid surprises and early backorders. Does the coverage report show adequate inventory to cover the first four weeks, which is 50% or more of the drop for most catalog business?

- In the second or third week of a promotion, reproject the number of units that will be sold, and note the effect that early sales numbers may have on other promotions featuring the item.

- In the third week, communicate the color/size sales distribution for the early results.

- Calculate 90% or another high percentage of your estimate of total demand for each item for the promotion.

- After two more weeks of selling, assuming that the product sales curve holds, accept the remainder of the merchandise.

- This means writing multiple purchase orders for the initial receipt and for subsequent deliveries, with the result that you can typically cover the first four to six weeks of selling and avoid a stock-out.

Multichannel merchants who treat inventory management as a strategic objective will improve customer service and reduce inventory at the same time they improve efficiency and profitability in warehouse operations. The route to developing such an inventory management strategy follows industry best practices, combining information across channels from planning, forecasting, and sales history to develop optimal inventory management processes.

Effective Liquidation

No matter how thoroughly your merchants plan or how accurately they forecast, overstocks will still happen. Overstocks are a natural part of merchandising, the final step in managing inventory left over because, for whatever reason, the forecasting didn't work. Minimizing overstocks is of course the first goal, but liquidating overstocks must be an integral part of the business process.

Sometimes overstocks may represent the emotional investments of a merchandiser or an entrepreneurial owner in his belief that the product would eventually sell. This kind of thinking can relegate overstocks to a sort of warehouse purgatory where they linger far too long. Best practice shows that cutting the retail price as soon as you're sure it's a slow seller is the most effective way to free up invested cash and gain the highest cost recovery.

Effective liquidation management involves determining which methods (Website, phone clearance, sale catalogs, stores, warehouse sales, inserts) are most effective at recovering merchandise costs, which methods are best suited for liquidating different quantities of merchandise, and how those methods can be used in concert if necessary.

The High Cost of Being on Backorder

	($ per Order)
CSR and phone line costs	$0.87
Pick/Pack/Ship labor costs	$0.58
Freight-Out	$3.50
Packing and shipping supplies	$1.05
Backorder notification costs	$0.50
Cancellation-CSR and phone line costs	$0.87
Total cost of one backordered item	$7.37
Times number of backordered items	40,000
TOTAL COST OF BACKORDERS	$294,8000

Costs not included in backorder:

- Prospecting
- Merchandising (expedited backorders)
- Returns (late shipments)
- Lost margin opportunities
- Added freight-in (air freight)
- Potential lost customers or ill will

Key Merchandise Metrics For Direct Marketers

	High Fashion	Reorderable Apparel	Gifts/ Housewares	Business Supplies
Initial order fill (%)	70-80	80-90	85-95	95-98
Final order fill (%)	90-95	95-99	96-100	99-100
Returns (net %)	20-40	10-20	2-12	< 2
Cancels (%)	4-8	3-6	2-5	< 2
Annual turnover (%)	4-7	3-7	4-6	5-10

10 Ways To Improve Vendor Quality Control

By Curt Barry

Quality Circles, Total Quality Management, Dr. Deming's 14 Point Theory and Six Sigma are all various programs aimed at improving quality in an organization. They have been successfully implemented in many corporations, but have failed to attract a following in the direct-to-customer fulfillment industry. Major reasons for this are the complexity and resources required to implement these highly touted quality control programs.

If you are seeking ways to improve your vendor quality control without having to dive headlong into a new way of doing business, take heart. There is an option that relies on the basics of upholding merchandise quality. The following are ten proven strategies for improving your vendor quality control program. These techniques also can be used to design such a program if you do not have one in place today.

1. Get accurate item specifications.

Both the catalog retailer and the vendor should have something in writing that accurately depicts each product's specifications, including important factors such as representing colors as accurately as possible and using the correct sizes and measurements. The catalog retailer should specify these standards.

This step is even more important if you have a unique product. Apparel items, for instance, must have detailed specifications, because it is critical to ensure that your customers are getting what they expect. Many return codes that list "not as pictured" as the return reason are caused simply by depicting an item in your catalog inaccurately. Eliminate that problem, and you likely eliminate a number of your returns.

2. Write a vendor compliance manual.

Vendor compliance means that product arrives from a vendor as it should—in proper condition and delivered in the agreed-upon manner. In addition to product quality, compliance standards that vendors must meet include packaging and shipping requirements, advanced shipping notices, master case and inner case, case labeling, product packaging and polybag specifications, accounting and paperwork requirements, logistics requirements and routing guides, scheduling and statistical sampling requirements, to name just a few.

Many operations don't have a good vendor compliance manual, but admit they should have one. This document lays out the details of how you and your vendors will handle each and every step in the product fulfillment relationship. While creating such a manual requires a bit of an investment in time, it can save a lot of headaches later on. When questions arise as to how to handle situations with vendors, you've already determined your company's position on the issues - it's in your manual! For example, when it comes to bar codes, the manual may specify to vendors what type of bar codes should be used, their location on the package, and whether they need to be human-readable.

Other topics a manual should cover include service expectations, packing and shipping instructions, invoicing, chargebacks and reasons, packing list information, purchase order and other forms, trans-

portation, labeling, palletizing, shipping carton identification and labeling, ship-alone carton specifications.

3. Establish good vendor relationships.

This sounds like a no-brainer — it's not. You're probably dealing
with hundreds of vendors, and it is important to establish clear, two-
way communication with each of them. Mutual site visits can be an
effective tool to promote understanding. For example, to facilitate
good working relations with vendors, a large multichannel retailer
held an open house recently at which it spent half a day showing all
the company's vendors through the different parts of the warehouse
and demonstrating how product was handled from receiving through
shipping. If you deal with a large number of vendors, it makes sense
to concentrate on those who supply the majority of your products.

It is important to create a contact list for your vendors so they can ask
questions and resolve problems by type of issue (e.g., product questions, chargebacks, accounts payable, traffic, etc.). In turn, your vendors should provide a single point of contact to whom you can direct
questions concerning quality or performance. Establishing such a
communications protocol is critical to streamlining the process.

4. Use vendor scorecards in the review process.

Develop a scorecard to measure and evaluate the performance of your
vendors. Used on an ongoing basis, a scorecard enables you to rank
your vendors-for example, as level A, B and C. These rankings can
then help you determine how often you need to inspect and sample
product shipments from those vendors: An A-level or "best"-ranked
vendor is not going to require the same level of scrutiny as is a B-level
vendor.

Some catalogs are extending the evaluation programs to include performance standards such as on-time delivery, product design, knowledge of the market segment, price competitiveness, and packaging and paperwork accuracy.

Make vendor review a part of the merchandise ordering cycle. Schedule a planned vendor-review process to coincide with placing orders for product. It is a great time to review performance and gain commitments for improvement while using the leverage of the purchase order.

5. Set up correction and remedy procedures.

You should clearly define the process and time for vendors to undertake any necessary corrections if your product or quality specifications are not met. Both parties should agree in advance on the steps to correct any continuing problems, as well as penalties if the issues are not resolved within a specific period of time.

Define the amount and method of applying vendor chargebacks when entering into a contract with a vendor, and record this information in the compliance manual. Depending on the problem, the correction process should be given some "teeth" to provide escalating steps toward improving quality.

6. Push compliance upstream.

Wherever possible, push the quality control program to your vendor facilities rather than to your receiving dock. For example, it is helpful if you can participate in inspections and approvals of product before they are shipped.

vendor site. The more work they can do at their end, the less you have to do in your warehouse.

7. Invest in infrastructure and gain management support.

To implement and conduct a vendor quality control program successfully, you'll need some dedicated infrastructure: computer systems, inspection equipment, fixtures, space, staffing, and travel expenses must be allocated to the program. In addition, keep in mind that it is impossible to implement a successful program of any kind without complete buy-in and support from top management. This is required not only to obtain finances to purchase the necessary infrastructure but also for the program to benefit from an ongoing commitment to its objectives. Vendor compliance cannot be enforced on a token basis.

8. Hire outside expertise where needed.

If the expertise you require is not available within your company, you should consider going outside and hiring people familiar with vendor quality control programs. Often, you'll actually save money by hiring outside help. There are industry experts available for hire in a huge variety of areas, from product sampling and quality testing to instituting vendor compliance standards and shipping programs.

9. Use a routing guide for inbound freight.

Often overlooked, inbound freight costs are among the top eight operational expenses for catalog and retail operations. Inbound freight costs an average 2% - 4% of gross sales for most direct marketers. One way to control these expenses is to have vendors ship freight collect using a pre-determined list of carriers, known as a routing guide. The latter is often combined with a vendor compliance manual.

In most cases the retailer, not the vendor, should be responsible for carrier selection and routing. In my experience, "best practice" companies allow little or no prepaid freight.

10. Don't forget drop-ship controls.

Vendors who drop ship to your customers require a slightly different type of control. There are software systems available that can track drop-ship performance and order status information. Having some degree of control over the service levels being met by your vendors in drop shipping is critical.

You still need a type of system in place to make sure the order gets to the customer, even though it doesn't physically go through your hands. You may have to pre-approve the vendors, see a certain number of samples, or institute some other measure of control with regard to drop shipping.

Implementing a vendor quality control program - and enforcing it consistently - is not easy, but its potential benefits make the effort worthwhile. Such a program can keep your overall costs in line, improving your bottom line and at the same time enhancing long-term customer satisfaction and the lifetime value of your customers.

Direct
Commerce
Systems

ERP Software In The Multichannel World

By Paul Sobota

Multichannel business managers frequently voice the desire to have one system or software package that is capable of managing the entire enterprise, encompassing all functional areas. Enterprise resources planning (ERP) systems have been available for years. Because the multichannel phenomenon—traditional brick-and-mortar businesses reaching into direct marketing, and traditional direct-to-customer companies developing brick-and-mortar stores as well as a Web presence—is so recent, it has in many cases outstripped the ability of software vendors to keep pace.

Having a single computer system control all functional areas in a business and use a common customer, inventory, order, and item database makes perfect sense, and the potential synergy between channels and the ability to maximize the customer experience are clear opportunities. Unfortunately, the search for and implementation of such a solution has frequently proved difficult.

The push to provide an overall multichannel solution has generally manifested itself in two ways. Traditional ERP vendors, whose genesis was in manufacturing, have tried to develop functionality geared to the specific needs of multichannel companies. Existing niche vendors in the direct-to-customer or retail worlds are trying to broaden their offerings to include more functional areas and look more like true ERPs. Both approaches have met with limited success so far. In general, niche or best-of-breed solutions fit more complex environments, while the ERP solutions better fit the very broad but less complex environments.

Size matters

There are many interpretations and definitions of "ERP" floating around. One of the clearest is that an ERP is a business management system that integrates all facets of the business, including planning (merchandise, staff, growth), manufacturing, sales, marketing, inventory control, fulfillment and replenishment, customer service, finance, and human resources. The system attempts to integrate all departments and functions across a company into a single computer system that serves independent departments' needs.

Many existing ERP packages are geared to larger businesses with multinational or broad business control needs. Many ERP systems have come from the manufacturing world and are now being developed to handle the very different operational requirements of the multichannel retail world. The relatively unique and complex nature of multichannel retail, combined with the large numbers of small and medium-sized multichannel businesses, has helped to create a void between traditional, deeply functional niche systems vendors and the functionality provided by ERP vendors. Finding an ERP solution with deep niche functionality geared to a medium-sized multichannel business can be an enormous challenge. But conversely, finding a niche player with deep functionality that can manage an entire multichannel enterprise is an equally difficult proposition.

Recent ERP market trends

ERP vendors face several obstacles in their effort to address the opportunities seemingly presented by the multichannel business market. The focus of ERP marketing has traditionally been on large companies willing to invest significant funds.

ERP vendors trying to enter mid-tier markets in retailing have been met with resistance from potential customers concerned about the level of service attention they will receive after implementation and about the lack of industry expertise on the part of the ERP vendors. There are many examples of ERP implementations failing—for many reasons. Considerations of scale, cost, and the time required for implementation have led to customer resistance to ERP vendors. Companies commonly fail to realize the level of discipline required to implement and use an ERP successfully. Most ERP installations follow a "Big Bang" approach, since the functionality is usually far reaching and encompasses many functional areas. Another drawback is that the installation time for major systems can be 12 to 18 months or even longer. (For example, two recent installations of ERPs in the food industry were so difficult that the businesses missed major selling seasons and product sales were months behind schedule.)

A good fit for an ERP would be in a far-reaching company with somewhat basic requirements desirous of having a single system to fully integrate all company information and data. Many ERPs are developing features that acknowledge the need for niche software by making it easier to integrate the two.

What about the competition? The sheer pace of recent acquisitions and consolidations in the software industry have made it difficult for niche systems vendors to effectively integrate suites of products into one unified approach with a clearly defined target market. Niche vendors who have deep, specialized functionality are beginning to compete successfully against the larger, more all-encompassing ERPs in the mid-market arena. And a recent trend in the systems market is for multichannel businesses to combine the niche, best-of-breed approach with an overall ERP solution.

Enterprise solutions

SAP

SAP, the world' largest business software company, has an ERP Retail solution that incorporates e-commerce with its customer relationship management (CRM) solution that allows users to analyze sales by channel. For direct marketers who also utilize catalog as a sales channel, however, SAP seems to have a disconnect related to specific functionality that is needed for catalogs. The solution lacks the list segmentation, source coding, catalog, drop, merchandise, square inch, contribution to profit functions required to analyze the success of mailing files, house and rented, and catalog promotions.

There are multichannel retailers, including ones that sell through a catalog, that are using SAP but they are also using specific direct-to-customer (DTC) software to set up, manage customer orders, fulfill, and analyze catalog promotions.

SAP also has an integration product, NetWeaver, with many different types of functionality, including the ability to link disparate systems. This would be one way to integrate sales from another application, such as catalog, and have this data flow into the SAP Retail solution for merchandise analysis. However, NetWeaver does not address a key element that catalogers measure, which is demand. As SAP and other ERP systems continue to evolve, in order to be true multichannel solutions they will need to adapt their software to include the functionality that is needed by those multichannel retailers who have a catalog sales channel.

SAP has another ERP software offering, Business One, for small to mid-sized companies. With SAP's acquisition of Triversity point-of-sale (POS) software and its integration to Business One ,which also includes an e-commerce module, a small to mid-sized company has a real solution to explore. Once again, however, if your company has a catalog sales channel there is no specific functionality to support this sales channel. Since Business One integration with Triversity is relatively new, it will be interesting to see how its catalog functionality progresses as new clients embrace this software.

Datavantage/CommercialWare

These two companies, along with their parent company, MICROS Systems, are taking a unified, integrated approach to bringing together all of their many retail and direct applications. In 2006 Commercial-Ware, one of the leading direct-to-customer software providers, was acquired by Datavantage. Datavantage is an industry leader in retail and point-of-sale applications. Between these companies the objective is to fully integrate their application suites (CWSerenade, cross-channel and direct; Xstore, JAVA-based, open standard, database-agnostic; Enterprise JAVA Merchandising, Web-based merchandise management solution with merchandise planning, purchasing, and distribution; Relate Retail, with CRM functionality for marketing and loyalty clubs; XBR Analytics). Implementation will involve a pre-planned set of parameters that will allow the user company to install an integrated set of applications more quickly than best-of-breed applications have been installed in the past. The company expects to have its first user live this summer. In the fall, all of the related companies will adopt the MICROS name.

Escalate

Escalate Retail's vision is to continue to develop specialized applications with a focus on direct businesses, e-commerce, retail management, and point of sale that can be implemented either as stand-alone applications or fully integrated. Continued development of service-oriented-architecture (SOA) will allow Escalate Retail to develop functionality, such as payment processing, shipping, pricing and promotions, that can be utilized by any or all of Escalate's suite of products. The aim is not to be a broad-based ERP application, but to be a best-in-class application for multichannel businesses with direct (Ecometry), retail (GERS), and e-commerce (Blue Martini) channels that wish to enhance their customer relationship and experience. Customers looking for an application that can support all aspects of the business with a single system need to understand that some functionality, such as financials, will still require a third-party application for AP and GL when they deploy the Escalate Retail Ecometry Commerce Suite.

Best of both worlds

A long-standing subject of debate is whether to try and combine best-of-breed niche software solutions or to employ an enterprise solution. At the moment, it appears that a blurring of industry definitions in the multichannel arena is occurring as some best-of-breed vendors try to expand their traditionally deep functionality to broader areas, while ERP vendors are deepening their traditionally broader offerings.

It will always be easier to match specific or unique requirements with a niche solution, but the integration of several of these packages is an issue. Attempts are being made to ease the burden with middleware development. In addition, some ERP vendors are now acknowledging the requirement for niche software and are facilitating integration with their solutions.

The search, selection, and implementation of an ERP for a multichannel company is a complex and difficult task. Since the welfare of a business depends on an effective system to control the business, the risk of making the wrong decision is significant.

We believe that ultimately ERPs will become more commonplace in the direct-to-customer, multichannel industry. The good news is, assuming that newer versions of ERPs are affordable, this increased competition will give companies more system product choices.

Here are a few suggestions for anyone considering the purchase of an ERP solution:

1. Make sure you do all of the homework required.
2. Keep in mind that the "Devil is in the details"
3. More options are rapidly being developed, so keep an open mind.
4. Strong training and discipline are required for successful implementation.
5. Insure that the ERP is flexible enough to meet future, as-yet-unknown requirements
6. Have a well–thought-out five-year plan to minimize future surprises.

The battle rages on but the options are changing.

Case studies: Different Approaches

Here are four examples of what large direct marketers are doing. We were asked to keep their names and the systems anonymous.

Large after-market direct seller of auto parts

The company looked at several ERPs but finally selected one of the leading direct-to-customer systems because of the large and expensive number of modifications that the ERP would have required (estimated costs over $2 million) in order to do the basics of marketing (capture, validation and analysis of source coding), inventory percent complete forecasting, drop-ship vendor network to dozens of vendors, profitability, and other management reporting, and to interface to the company's Internet shopping site.

Gift & book retailer with 150 stores and major catalog and eCommerce site

The company has implemented Oracle's Retail Suite. The implementation took 24 months—three times the estimated man-hours for implementation.

Pros: It has one of the most powerful database functionalities in the market—a significant advantage. Oracle is a good launching pad for other applications and provides good accounting; order management and its inventory visibility is OK; overall it has broad functionality. The genesis of Oracle is in manufacturing and shows in its detailed functionality in certain areas.

Cons: System is weak in some multichannel areas of functionality (call center credit card, backorders, multichannel inventory channelization). The WMS is really a locater system, which makes it a weak link for multichannel fulfillment. There are different user interface processes (Web and fixed), possibly due to multiple systems being put together under one umbrella. Basic reports are numerous but very generic. The functional gap was greater than expected in some areas, requiring additional modifications to meet business needs.

Major retailer with fast-growing eCommerce site and major catalog

This company is in the process of replacing its legacy call center and customer service applications with an ERP and CRM application. The retailer intends to take a best-of-breed approach, interfacing to its commercial WMS and direct merchandise planning and forecasting systems. For the stores the company will continue to use a commercial retail system. This is an expensive multi-year implementation.

Major direct marketer and retailer of gifts with hundreds of stores

The business is installing an ERP for most of its functional applications, but has chosen to keep its full-function commercial WMS and some other legacy applications. The ERP's warehousing system did not give as much inventory control in the distribution center as the WMS.

ERP Requirements Checklist by Function

It's a major proposition to find, install, and work with an ERP system. Below are guidelines to consider as you go through the process of making a choice.

General

1. The discipline required to utilize an ERP is significant. The integration and dependency of the process on accurate and timely input and maintenance of data is critical. Bad data in the ERP environment can be disastrous to the entire organization.
2. Are all modifications part of future releases, or are you going to be supporting a customized system?

E-commerce

1. ERP e-commerce software has been better suited in the past for B2B, and not specifically B2C.
2. The use of an ERP e-commerce module as an independent software package is not recommended. Such a module works best in conjunction with use of an entire ERP system.
3. Some ERP vendors are purchasing niche e-commerce solutions

and integrating them to their package.

4. Some are beginning to offer on-demand or software-as-a-service types of e-commerce services.

5. Some larger ERP solutions are reaching down into the medium and small markets to attempt to provide solutions

Direct Marketing

1. Does the ERP have a direct orientation for the data—multiple channels, promotion codes, source coding and reporting, catalog drops, circulation, validation of products, and source codes by offer, etc.?

2. Review your current system to see how well the ERP will accomplish direct-oriented data and analysis.

Merchandising and Inventory Control

1. What are the management reporting and merchandise analyses that your business uses or needs? Are these catalog- and Internet-oriented functions available from the ERP vendor?

2. Is there assortment planning by catalog/drop and Internet?

3. Does the system have the appropriate direct-oriented data for catalog planning—demand, backorders, sales, square-inch measurements for space use, and costs by category, class, product, SKU, page/picture, price range? Or will you need a data warehouse?

4. Is there percent complete forecasting by category and product for in-season forecasting?

5. What end-of-promotion and seasonal analysis is there, and is it direct-oriented?

Call Center

1. Ability to note and follow up on customer inquiry and complaints

2. Backorder tracking and FTC analysis
3. Interface of telephone system to order management system for CTI (screen pop ups of customer accounts)
4. Pre-paid liability tracking for mail order customers (payment for orders received versus outstanding back orders)

Fulfillment—key issues to evaluate with ERP WMS functionality

1. Real-time inventory management
2. Multiple choices in operating procedures such as picking
3. Virtual and/or physical inventory separation by channel
4. Complete use of bar code technology throughout the warehouse
5. Supports both pick/pack for direct and store replenishment for retail channel processes
6. Provides interfaces to various warehouse automation opportunities
7. Captures and reports productivity measures by individual, department or function, and warehouse
8. Supports multiple warehouse facilities
9. Provides for international shipping capabilities
10. Provides both min–max and demand replenishment processes for pick slots
11. Cross-dock capabilities for store distribution and backorder processing
12. Utilizes rate shopping process to minimize freight costs
13. Full-functional inbound and outbound freight management

Junction Solutions

Junction Solutions has built its suite based on Microsoft Dynamics AX (a widely installed ERP System). For illustration purposes, think of the functionality in three levels. Microsoft develops and enhances the dynamics level of distribution software. Junction Solutions develops and maintains a second level of functionality for the direct and retail marketplace. The third level is for customized company application functionality. Clearly, one of the objectives is to cater to companies that need customized business functionality. The total application suite includes call center, e-commerce, POS, and store operations (Junction Solutions has acquired ISS, which has retail POS applications installed in large retailers such as Target, Dillards and Best Buy), a warehouse management system, and distribution, logistics, and business intelligence. Retail planning and merchandising are being added this year. Junction is investing heavily in service-oriented architecture. The platform is .NET.

As with Datavantage/CommercialWare (see article) the influx of capital from its parent company is helping to strengthen the product offering. Junction Solutions seems to have a potential early leg up based on its true ERP product offering for larger businesses. Ultimately, with such a young product offering and customer base, time will prove who is on the right track.

Scripted Demos And The OMS

By Brian Barry

Q: We have been investigating replacing our order management system, and we have had vendors in to demonstrate their systems. While we have spent a lot of time, we don't ever seem to see the whole system or the particular features that are critical to our business.

A: Two words: scripted demos.

First, there are two types of demos. The first type, lasting one to two hours, is used to get the general feel for a system early in the search process. What you get is a high-level overview of a couple of system functions. The second type of demonstration, which lasts six-to-eight hours, is the kind we'll focus on. This longer demo is used to select the finalists after vendors have responded to your request for proposal.

Remember, the job of the salesman is to show you the strengths of the system he's selling. Your job is to make sure that you have done your due diligence to determine which system fits your business best. In working with our clients on hundreds of order management and warehouse management systems projects, we have found the most effective way to make that determination is to literally script what it is that you want the vendor to demonstrate.

By scripting the demo we mean getting the vendors to show you the features and functions of the software at a level of detail that allows you understand how it would fit your business. You take control of the demo content, the agenda, the data to be presented, and the amount of time the vendor will spend on various subsystems.

Here are some guidelines:

- Who are the key department users? They should prepare a list of specific items or functionality they want the vendor to demonstrate from the RFP responses (e.g., promotion set-up, blanket purchase orders, item master, quantity price break discounts, etc.).

- Start with your user requirements. What were the essential functions that you needed? Which do you think are unique to your business? These may be loyalty clubs, discounting, carrier rate shopping, bill-me-later, product numbering schemes, etc.

- Make sure that the vendor has your media (catalogs, inserts, Website URL, etc.) and uses data that you have prepared to demo his system. Dummied-up customer records, products, and SKUs, different discount options (free freight; buy one, get one free), kitting/de-kitting, product numbering, length of fields (e.g., name, address, SKU).

- Write out a literal script and a time agenda, including the order of topics to be demonstrated. If you don't conduct the demonstrations in the same way and following the same sequence, you won't be able to compare one system to another. This is a major reason for taking control of the demo. You should recognize that of course the vendor has his own agenda—ask for it in advance, view it, and only use that portion of it that benefits the system selection process. Let me give you an example. Vendors always want to start with a detailed background of their business. You do need to understand the company, its market, who the installed customer base is, and so on. But can't you do that over the phone or through Webinars? Remember that you are doing the demo after presenting your requirements and receiving a response back from the vendor. The vendors who are going to conduct these demos are already on the short list.

- Assign a "scribe' to document the key pluses and minuses of each system as well as vendor follow-up items. Department users should be responsible for keeping track of any changes, follow-up items, or feature/function that appears to be a strength or weakness. Don't rely on the vendor to take the notes. Don't think that you will remember or be able to recall what you saw after the fact.

- Use the demo to validate the vendor responses in the RFP. You should go through any major requirements that you questioned or didn't understand, or any for which you want to see how the function works.

- Update the RFP response with any changes or new impressions based on the demo.

- Mark results on a score card. After the vendor leaves, get the participants together to score their impressions on each functional area, A–F, and enter key observations on a form. For what functions do key users need more explanation? What are their concerns?

- Follow up with a memo to vendors of items they agreed to research, and include any outstanding concerns and questions. Some questions may require an additional demonstration of a specific function or functions, this should be easily accommodated by the vendors through a Webinar.

The better prepared you are and the more firmly you take control of the demo, the better you can ensure that the system fits your business.

The Art Of Data Conversion

By Paul Sobota

Q: We are in the process of planning our file conversion as we implement our new catalog management system. Our vendor is telling us that they normally don't write a file conversion program for most files. What's your recommendation?

A: Today's comprehensive order management system performs integrated functionality for order entry, customer service, order processing, warehousing, marketing and merchandising.

There are literally hundreds of tables and files in these systems that have to be converted or built from scratch manually. These range from promotional tables, shipping tables to the more complex customer files, item masters and purchase order files.

For smaller businesses, the better approach is to minimize the automated file conversion. For larger companies (meaning tens of thousands of customers and products) it will be a blend of build manually and program file conversation.

The reasons are:

- Converting years of history often result in many file integrity problems because the data is not consistent over long periods of time. Needless to say it takes many more passes through the data and it may still not be totally corrected;

- Conversion programs take time to write and test. Many of the new systems files and tables can be set up faster manually than writing programs and converting files;

- Setting up files has also proven to be a good way of training departmental users in what the new system will require in terms of maintenance. It gives you familiarity with the new system at a detail level. If you attempted to convert all files the users will never understand early what the system requires.

For larger businesses, it may be more compelling to look at automating a larger share of the file conversion. But we would still advise that this should not be taken to extreme.

Some Guidelines:

- Most companies under estimate the time required to develop specs, program and test file conversion and using copies of subsets of the live file in training.

- Don't try to machine convert too much data – too many years back. How much history do you need to convert?

- Look at using your marketing service bureau to be a source of hygiened customer data. Get them involved with the file conversion early to see how they can assist you. If you use them, you'll end up sending them the files once the conversion programs are tested, several days before the "go live". This will assure that you'll have an update, hygiene customer data file. Merge/purge to eliminate duplicates just before the conversion. Address correction and NCOA would be performed.

- Take into account the data file problems that multiple years of data may have. System created problems, changes in coding of transactions or tables, etc.

- Consider the amount of time required to make the file conversion during "go live". Obviously, you don't test with the live data file. Initially test with a copy of selected records from the files. Selected records which are illustrations of as many conditions as you can identify. Then, do a conversion volume test to see how long the actual file conversion will take. This is especially crucial with large files (e.g. customers and item master) being loaded to a relational data base.

- Schedule sufficient time to humanly review data. Can't look at every record but you need to sample the converted file sufficiently to know the file conversion programs are working correctly. The user departments should all be involved in reviewing samples in the files they use. If you only review a few accounts you are taking a high risk.

- Plan out the final days of the conversion. There will be the need to begin the file conversion a few days in advance of the "go live" date. Most businesses can not shut down the business during the file conversion, so you need to figure out how to update the key files during the "go live". How will you continue to process new customer orders and returns, add new products, etc.? Need to go back and update the files during the "go live".

Can you keep your old system operational for some period of time to answer inquiries and compare records? Remember a very high percentage of inquiries and complaints happen in the first 90 to 120 days after the sale or return and then inquiries drop off quickly Does all customer data need to be on the new system back 10 years? But for the for marketing purposes we don't want to lose customer purchase activity and promotional history.

File Build Versus Convert

In our consulting practice we look at each company's file conversion and its file data objectively. But here are some generalizations about the types of files and whether should be built manually versus converted.

These are the files that are typically file converted with programs customer files, item masters, customer order and return history, inventory files, purchase orders, subset of item master for WMS system, item locations, etc.

The majority of files and tables are set up manually by user departments. These include promotions, source codes, sales tax, shipping & handling, files which govern business rules (system control values which determine the functions of the system), open orders (keying the data gives you experience with order entry and all the order coding), general ledger chart of accounts, merchandise hierarchy (div, dept, class,) and employee files.

Types of files could go either way – build or convert - accounts receivables.

There are some types of files – like the historical promotions - that aren't converted. The results may be sent to a data warehouse, spreadsheet or marketing data base.

Summary

Get with user management and get an early start on planning the conversion. Realistically, consider what it will take to convert files by program versus building them manually and giving the user departments more experience with the new system's maintenance.

E-commerce Platforms And Solutions

By Tocky Lawrence

Any company choosing an e-commerce platform is faced with a bewildering number of choices. Determining which of these solutions best fits your needs is no longer as simple as having your local Internet provider develop a Web page with navigation and some type of shopping-cart functionality.

E-commerce solutions have evolved to include core functionality for navigation, shopping cart, checkout, shipping and handling, and taxes and some level of integration to an order management system (OMS), an enterprise resource planning (ERP) system, or a warehouse management system (WMS). Then there are the Web 2.0 options: rich media with audio and visual tools, customer product reviews, social networking, blogs. Newer technology also provides functionality for options such as mouse-over (move the mouse over an image and the description will display without the user's having to click on the image), drag and drop (simply drag the item to the shopping cart without leaving the current page), and one-page checkout.

Given this array of possibilities, how do you determine the best e-commerce platform for your business? Here are a few guidelines:

Treat your search as a system selection project. Too often companies have viewed e-commerce as a separate part of their business. In reality e-commerce has become integral to multichannel marketers. Today multichannel companies report that on average 35%-45% of their business comes through the Web.

You should view your search for an e-commerce platform the same way you would a search for a new OMS or WMS. Spend time up front to understand what the e-commerce solution should provide, determine the project team, and develop a budget and a timeline.

Develop your vision. Before you can determine what the e-commerce platform should provide, you need to know what you want your Website to do and how you want to use it from a conceptual standpoint. The project team needs to have a clear vision of how the site should look and function, what the growth objectives are, and who the target customer is.

To develop the conceptual vision, you'll need to involve user management from all departments, including the contact center, merchandising, and the stores in addition to marketing, IT, and online. As a management team, what is their collective vision for the Website and how it should serve the customer? How do they want your customer to view the business? If you have stores, do they want site visitors to feel as if they've entered one of them? What types of marketing efforts need to be included? How do you want to display merchandise? These are just a few of the questions that go into developing a vision for an e-commerce platform solution.

Define your requirements. This is a natural extension of developing your vision. What do you want the site to do? What type of functionality do you want? Everybody has shopping-cart technology — is there anything in particular that you need yours to do, such as personalization or cross-selling? What sort of Web analytics features do you need?

Determine the degree of customization and flexibility you may want. Customization may take the form of something as simple as the ability to change promotions — offering a special discount on a given day, for instance. Or you might want to be able to change elements such as site navigation. How flexible does the solution really need to be? Don't get mired in jargon and functional possibilities. Concentrate instead on how your new site will produce sales or increase inquiries that lead to sales.

Keep integration requirements in mind. Implementing an e-commerce platform with all the bells and whistles will fall short if your OMS or ERP system can't effectively communicate with the site.

Decide whether you want to build or buy. Building your own e-commerce platform historically provided a competitive advantage in the marketplace, as packaged e-commerce solutions were expensive and basic. Many companies viewed their online business as different from anyone else's and thought their uniqueness required a homegrown platform.

Times have changed, however, and companies now realize that the real differentiator for their Website is the look and feel, the effectiveness of its onsite search, and its merchandising (the presentation as well as the actual goods). Today many e-commerce platforms offer similar basic features and functionalities.

While the build solution ultimately offers custom fit and control, using resources to build basic functions such as product catalog management, merchandising features, campaign management, and shopping-cart functionality can put a company at a disadvantage because of the amount of time needed to develop the underlying technology layers for functionality and the integration points to your existing systems. It commonly takes 12-24 months to design, develop, and build an e-commerce solution from scratch. Then there's the matter of finding and keeping experienced staff to build the solution. The question arises whether your company is better off using its resources to support its core competency rather than to develop a solution that already exists.

As the second generation of e-commerce evolves, more marketers are opting to buy packaged or custom software. Platform programs generally encompass features such as visualization (product rotation and zoom), merchandising (marketing products based on customer preference, past history, or best-sellers), and personalization (offering the customer marketing opportunities based on purchasing patterns). Vendors have built more functionality into their platforms to handle the basic online selling features for product catalog management, merchandising, campaign management, and shopping-cart functionality. Another advantage to using a packaged solution is that the vendor provides upgrades to the core functionality.

Some vendors are incorporating Web 2.0 features into their solutions while at the same time offering integration to third-party software (best-of-breed solutions) that can handle a more in-depth customer interaction. Buying an e-commerce platform that provides all the required core functionality as well as the ability to use best-of-breed applications and custom services is generally considered the optimal solution. The goal is to achieve a balance between the e-commerce solution and the number of best-of-breed applications, since maintaining multiple applications for the long term can increase maintenance costs.

If you decide to buy, choose between a licensed solution or software as a service (SaaS). With licensed software, you purchase the e-commerce software package and host the solution in-

ternally or externally at an outsourced hosting facility.
Licensing for a packaged software solution is normally structured on a
per-user or per-CPU basis and typically requires an up-front investment of $400,000 and up. Annual maintenance costs usually fall in the
range of 15%-22% of the license cost. The license model also requires
an investment in server hardware and database software.

Vendors offering packaged e-commerce solutions have built core features and functionality into their solutions but provide the flexibility to
customize a Website's look and feel. The licensed model is typically
used by midsize and large multichannel companies wanting absolute
control of their e-commerce platform. Benefits include the ability to
make changes as required, reduced time to introduce new features,
and the ability to integrate with best-of-breed technologies.

Purchasing licensed software is the more common solution. The SaaS,
or on-demand, model is gaining in popularity, however, especially
among businesses that do not want to commit the large up-front investment required by a licensed model. This is particularly true of
small and midsize companies that don't require complete control of
their platform.

An on-demand e-commerce platform provides a company with the use
of a vendor's solution for a flat monthly fee or a percentage of revenue. The vendor owns and hosts the software, which may exist on a
shared or nonshared environment. In a shared environment there is
one version of the software, and all clients share the code and server
resources. In the less common nonshared environment, the resources
are dedicated to a particular client.

Up-front setup fees for an on-demand solution can range from
$50,000 to $400,000, depending on the complexity and size of the
client's business. The flat-fee or revenue model is typically set up with

a tiered structure based on online revenue, site visits, or order volume. Fees are typically 1.5%-3% of sales.

Look at the pros and cons of hosting and managed services. Hosting means that you buy a solution and the necessary hardware and pay the vendor to put the hardware in its facility, where it will reside. In the managed-services model, you buy the hardware and the software, the vendor hosts the hardware, and you contract with the vendor to maintain the operating system and e-commerce software application.

Before you decide which model you want to use, you need to understand the vendor's concept of maintenance and updating; you also need to know your IT staff's ability to support hosting the solution internally or externally.

Seek a vendor you can partner with. When you're researching e-commerce companies, you want to find a vendor that will work actively with you. It's crucial to have that kind of relationship in order to be sure that you will have the support and maintenance you need.

Six Tips for Avoiding Common Pitfalls

Put your requirements in writing. Too often e-commerce solutions are built or customized based on verbal agreements — but what the vendor provides and the customer expects don't always match.

Conduct a request for proposal (RFP) process. This identifies to the vendor what your requirements are and establishes initial pricing.

Develop a three- to five-year budget scenario with up-front or startup costs, initial year investment, and subsequent years' investment. Include annual maintenance fees for hardware and software support. It's important to understand the total investment to determine which solution is best for your business.

Define a schedule or timeline. Many companies underestimate the time it takes from establishing requirements to implementation.

Formalize a project plan.

Be sure to schedule status updates on regular intervals.

A Sampling Of – e-commerce platform providers

There are many e-commerce platforms from which to choose — so many that we can't possibly compile a comprehensive list here. Below is information on some of the major providers.

ATG (Art Technology Group)
617-386-1000; www.atg.com
ATG offers a large suite of modules that complement its core ATG Commerce solution, including ATG Merchandising, ATG Campaign Optimizer, and ATG Outreach for e-mail and Web marketing. ATG offers both a licensed solution and an SaaS model, as well as hosting as an option.

Demandware
781-756-3700; www.demandware.com
One of the newer players, Demandware offers an SaaS model that includes installation, upgrades, and scaling. The solution gives marketers and merchandisers the ability to maintain promotions, site con-

tent, product information, and analytics. Demandware Studio provides the client the flexibility to customize the creative and functional design aspect with full control of design templates, business logic, and page flow.

Fry
800-379-6858; www.fry.com
Fry offers its Open Commerce Platform (OCP) as a paid-services engagement: Clients own the code, and Fry performs site development and maintenance. Fry's strong background and expertise in Web design along with OCP as the foundation provides a client with a highly customized solution.

GSI Commerce
610-491-7664; www.gsicommerce.com
GSI Commerce Core Technology Services is a combination of proprietary and third-party applications built to flexibly support features and functions on a common infrastructure while allowing each partner's solution to be customized to fit individual business needs. GSI Commerce allows partners to maintain the e-commerce solution through the use of promotions management, search management, catalog management, and content management. Along with its e-commerce platform, GSI offers an end-to-end solution including technology services, customer care, and fulfillment.

IBM Corp.
914-499-1900; www-306.ibm.com/software/websphere
IBM's Websphere Commerce comes in three variations: Websphere Commerce Enterprise for large, high-volume b-to-b and advanced b-to-c global businesses; Websphere Commerce Professional for online selling that incorporates personalized and cross-channel shopping; and Websphere Commerce-Express, which provides core capabilities for smaller companies.

MarketLive

877-341-5729; www.marketlive.com

MarketLive's MarketLive5 e-commerce platform is an end-to-end so-lution containing marketing, merchandising, customer loyalty, product management, site management, and order processing. It can deploy as a subscription-based, customizable shared-instance solution; as a hosted solution; or as an on-premises solution.

Microsoft Corp.

425-705-3739; www.microsoft.com/commerceserver/default.mspc

Microsoft's Commerce Server 2007 is designed to fully leverage ASP.NET 2.0. It has merchandising, catalog management, order proc-essing, and .NET smart client user interfaces.

Prosodie Interactive

866-544-9582; www.prosodieinteractive.com

Prosodie Commerce includes a merchandise tool and search engine optimization, affiliate marketing, loyalty program, and promotional options. It is available as a hosted dedicated solution or in a shared-server environment.

Vcommerce Corp.

480-922-9922; www.vcommerce.com

Vcommerce's eCommerce Storefront, an SaaS solution, provides mer-chandising, integrated analytics, search and guided navigation, predic-tive merchandising and personalization, and A/B testing. Vcommerce also offers order management, service, and fulfillment options.

Venda

480-922-9922; www.vcommerce.com

Venda's e-commerce solution is an SaaS solution that includes prod-uct and catalog management, merchant content management, self-service promotions, e-mail marketing campaigns, affiliate marketing, natural-language search engine functionality, and personalization.

Additional solutions to consider:

Amazon 866-557-2823
www.Amazonservices.com/aes

BroadVision 650-542-5100
www.broadvision.com

Competitive Computing 802-764-1700
www.competitive.com

Digital River 952-253-1234
www.digitalriver.com

eOne Group 402-970-6701
www.eonegroup.com

LaGarde 913-489-8000
www.storefront.net

NetSuite 650-627-1181
www.netsuite.com

SiteForm 773-334-8030
www.siteform.com

Warp 9 800-508-9339
www.warp9inc.com

Weblinc 215-925-1800
www.weblinc.com

Yahoo! Small Business 866-781-9246
smallbusiness.Yahoo.com/ecommerce

Get The Most From Your New Order Management System With A Post-Implementation Audit

By Brian Barry

Q: Our company installed our new order management system in the last 30 days. While we spent considerable time educating our users and completing the conversion, I'm concerned that we are learning how to manage our business with the new system too slowly. What should our plan of action be?

At F Curtis Barry & Company we often see that, even a year after purchasing and installing a comprehensive system, companies use maybe 25% to 35% of its potential functionality. Obviously, you'd hope that you'd get much higher use, since companies spend significant capital to purchase and install a new system. Historically, management doesn't look at how to increase the use of installed systems.

Having implemented order management and warehouse systems dozens of times, what we have found is that it often takes two to six months for the entire organization to make that cultural change to the new system. In the beginning weeks, they act like they're in slow motion.

The Solution

Your plan of action should be to do a post-implementation audit of all aspects of the conversion and system use. Well after the system implementation, an audit can help increase use of the system. A post-implementation audit will help you confer with the vendor and your people about how to get more out of the system – and make sure users have a complete understanding of the system in areas that have high personnel turnover.

A consultant, an auditor, or a management member can perform the audit objectively. (Keep in mind, there may be some sensitive issues if training or conversion didn't go as planned.) The audit should include all departments using the system, company management, your IT department, and the vendors. The goal is to consider all aspects of the implementation and obtain answers to the following:

- What is the open list of items left from the conversion?
- What problems is the company having with the new system?
- What people need to be retrained? Be sure all parties understand how to manage your business with the new system ("In the old system I had this, what do I use now?").
- What doesn't appear to be working?
- What don't you understand in the new system?
- Is management getting all the reports and analysis you expected? This is generally one of the major shortcomings.
- Are there some problems left from the file conversion? Data being converted is often not "very clean data".

Key Departmental Areas

To find these answers, your audit should consider the following issues:

Are there any customer-service impacts that need to be fast-tracked (e.g., order processing, returns/credit processing, abandonment rate, pick error rates)?

Even with a large amount of training, it takes the practical experience of performing daily work for the users to really understand all aspects of how the system is set up and needs to be managed. The company will need to get through the month-end and seasonal processes before you have mastered some systems.

What program problems are there? From the IT perspective, if it's is a radical change in platform or functionality, how well are they providing system availability? Is the help desk up to speed? Are printers and terminals in the right locations and in sufficient numbers? Are all the interfaces ready for non-daily activities (e.g., printers, merge/purge services, etc.)?

Did the vendors perform their duties in line with the written and verbal agreements? Did the conversion come off accurately? Are there still clean-up problems? In retrospect, how well did they manage the conversion with you? Did you get what you were promised in the pre-sales and negotiations?

In setting up systems today there are hundreds to thousands of software switches that determine the "system personality" and functionality. Are all of these set right? Are there some that need to be reconsidered?

From an integration or interface perspective, these data exchanges are often the most difficult to implement and debug. Are all these inter-departmental systems working correctly?

Order management systems and warehouse management systems have data feeds to accounting and general ledger. Are all the financial aspects of these systems working accurately?

Are there additional operations functions or processes that are needed, or should be investigated, to gain more productivity and to improve throughput?

What program modifications have been delayed and will now be scheduled as a subsequent phase? From your experience with the system, are these modifications and enhancements really necessary, or are there new functions, now that you understand the system, that you can use in their place.

From the perspective of company's standard operating procedures, are the procedures completed? What still needs to be done, or changed and updated, so that you have a way to educate future employees?

While you're doing this assessment, go back to your original objectives or feasibility study. Realistically, have you achieved (or will you achieve) the tangible dollar savings promised (e.g., personnel savings, inventory turnover)? Has the company gained the intangible benefits expected (e.g. customer service levels, ability to plan and analyze the business better)?

Create an Action Plan

Once you have completed this survey, you need to circulate the results to all parties and get their concurrence that this audit is in fact a complete list and all the points are valid. Showing the list to everyone, generally often means that the list gets smaller because people will help each other answer things by saying, "Here's how you can do that," or "I didn't find that to be true."

From this point you should develop an action plan to improve, reeducate, complete conversions, and take full advantage of additional

reporting and options that you decided to delay and determine a realistic schedule for further modifications and reports.

Remember that you're often treading on sensitive territory when
you're talking about individuals and how well they are doing their job
with the new system. Obviously, there may be a need for changes in
personnel or retraining which need to be shielded from the total group.

After getting concurrence with regard to the outstanding list, the next
step is to assign priorities, responsibilities, and due dates to be able to
follow up with everyone. Follow up with each management member
each week about their assigned areas in order to whittle down the list
and get this conversion totally behind you.

After you feel you've mastered the basic system, many vendors offer
more advanced education in certain specialized topic — oriented to
application, report writer, data warehousing.

Use a post-implementation audit to get a considerably higher use of
the system in which you have invested and achieve the savings and
benefits originally projected.

Systems Selection

By Brian Barry

Q: I am trying to select a new catalog management system that also includes warehouse functionality. After reading the brochures, talking with vendors, and participating in webinars with them, how do I make sense of all the information?

A: Software vendors have great brochures and Websites, but avoid narrowing your search down too quickly. Initial discussions and online demos will show you just a portion of what the software can do.

To begin, document your business requirements, listing each and every task that the new application needs to accomplish. Include any future needs and wishes as well. This allows you to send a detailed request for proposal (RFP) to each vendor. You can then evaluate their responses in a comparative format. No one can remember everything that a vendor's product is capable of, especially after reviewing several online demos. Get the vendors to respond by telling you what is actually available in their base applications rather than something that they will have to modify.

Next, sort through the vendors' responses and eliminate those that do not fit a high percentage of your requirements without modifications. If there seem to be a large number of modifications from all the vendors, you should ask yourself whether you are looking at the right group of vendors and if the requirements you documented truly what your business needs.

Look to reduce, if not completely rule out, the need for any modifications if possible. Narrow your choices down to two or three software vendors you believe are capable of supporting your business and bring the top two vendors in for scripted demos—your agenda for vendor presentations--keeping a third vendor "in reserve" just in case.

Base your scripted demos on business functions specific to your business that you want to be sure the vendor can perform. Remember, you control the software demonstration, and you decide what is important for your organization to view and understand.

To develop your scripted demos, work with each of your user departments to address their major concerns, reviewing in detail how the software can accomplish these requirements. Send the vendors examples of your catalogs, a link to your Website, and a list of functions you specifically want to have demonstrated, such as drop-shipping.

For the demos themselves, have each vendor walk through the entire business process, from creation of items and offers to writing purchase orders, receiving, and put-away. Ask the vendors to demonstrate the entire order entry process with multiple scenarios, including back-ordered items, ship alone, and multi-line and single-line orders. Follow an order through all of its processes from credit-card authorization through pick, pack, and ship. Don't forget returns and customer service issues that you encounter every day. Be sure you have a scribe who can write down the details of what works well and what does not. Also, there will inevitably be post-demo follow-up queries that you want to have documented and forwarded to the vendors for responses.

Ultimately you are trying to determine which vendor can be a long-term partner and assist you better with growing your business. No vendor is going to be a 100% fit, and you should scrutinize vendors that tell you either in the RFP or in the demo that they can support 100% of your requirements.

As soon as possible after each demo is completed, you will want the participants from each functional area in your business to provide a high-level scoring of the vendor's functionality. You will need to rank the pluses and minuses of the software demonstration in each functional area while they are still fresh in everyone's mind.

If at this point the scripted demos—and whatever immediate follow-up is necessary— have you comfortable with these vendors, it's time to take the next steps in finalizing your decision: reference checks and site visits.

When checking vendor references, ask to see the full customer list, not just the vendor's selected references. You want to make sure that you will not be either the largest or smallest client with a particular vendor. If you're the largest, you risk having to drag the vendor along in order to enhance the application fast enough to suit your growing business. If you're the smallest, you may not receive the level of attention you need from the support group. Call as many as possible of the vendor's customers that are of a similar size or have a product makeup similar to your company, as well as any other companies that you feel are leaders in the industry. It's a good idea to review any areas that you feel might pose a problem for your company and ask if the vendor's clients have had any issues in that area. Ask if they have to work around any of the vendor's functionality.

You are trying to confirm that you are headed down the right path in selecting the best possible partner for a long-term investment. Ask the references everything: Did the vendor complete the installation on time and within the budget? How are the software releases—are they full of bugs or pretty clean? How is the vendor's support? How active is the user group? How well does the vendor listen to its customer base?

Choose one or two of each vendor's clients to visit. Seeing first-hand how a similar business uses the application is very important. Here you can tell where the true work-arounds are and how efficiently customers are able to use the application. You will also get a much deeper perspective then you would from a phone conversation.

Hopefully at the end of this process you will have done all the homework and research you need to make a well-founded decision that will create a partnership with a vendor for many years to come.

Let Your Software Do Your Scheduling

By Tocky Lawrence

Scheduling staff for your customer contact center is much more than simply plugging your customer service representatives' names into time slots for each day of the week. It's an infinitely complex task. You have to factor in days off, vacations, skill sets, seniority, and individual availability against the needs of the entire center, call volumes, and fluctuations in volume based on catalog mailings, TV ads, and special promotions. Scheduling all these variables manually can take days – and can leave supervisory staff little time for other important tasks.

Doing a poor job of scheduling can have serious ramifications for your business. If your call center's seats aren't filled when you need them to be, your service levels will drop, your abandonment rate will rise, and ultimately, you'll lose sales and customer loyalty. On the other hand, if you have too many reps scheduled at a particular time, you can waste thousands of dollars and drive up your cost per call. With a scheduling system in place, staffing decisions can be made on the spot as problems unfold, instead of days or weeks later.

Up in the tower

With the scheduling software tools on the market today, there's no need for reps to acquire the skills of, say, Quasimodo. Prices for scheduling software base packages start as low as $30,000, and with all of the bells and whistles can push $100,000 or more. But the right software package will pay for itself in many ways. Most clients we've worked with report that their scheduling packages have reduced their staffing process time by 50% or more per week. Abandonment rates can also be reduced by 5% to 10%. Many software companies claim that their products will result in savings of 10% or more for labor expenses; however, based on our clients' experiences, we think reductions of 3% to 5% are more achievable.

Automating your schedule will also result in intangible benefits such as better employee retention through better scheduling, more time for supervisors to perform other tasks, and more effective hiring decisions. You'll begin to see how, after a few months, you will be managing the process of scheduling instead of just spending hour after hour producing schedules.

If you are running a call center with 25 seats or more and you have 24/7 operations, you are at the point where a scheduling package could make a significant difference in your weekly and monthly scheduling routine. In fact, if your operation has reached this size and you're not using scheduling software, someone in your organization is probably spending an inordinate amount of time producing inferior schedules.

Starting bell

There are many call center scheduling packages on the market, but not all are designed for direct-to-customer operations. It's wise to limit your search to packages that are designed for catalogs. Within this category, too, some packages are more limited than others. It's a good idea to have a sense of what the various vendors offer as you start out.

The telephone switch you use will influence your choice of vendor. These scheduling systems are independent from the telephone switch, which typically just forecasts calls, but the two must be compatible. Before you start to shop, review the specs of your current switch. Likewise, your personnel resources will be important in getting the most out of your scheduling software. Make sure you have personnel who have the skills necessary to learn and run the system.

As with many software packages, what you'll get out of your scheduling software is only as good as the data you put in. It's best to have at least one to two years of call history from your ACD. The system will need this information to configure the proper curves of incoming calls by day, week, season, and for events such as mailings and promotions. The more history you've got, the more accurate the scheduler's predictions will be.

Because call centers handle informational inquiries, catalog requests, complaints and other calls, it's important to look at overall call volumes and call-to-order ratios – not just order history – to get an accurate idea of your staffing needs. You'll also need to compile your call center's service goals, such as acceptable wait times and abandonment rates.

Bells and whistles

Scheduling software packages come with all sorts of options. Some of the latest versions interface with e-mail management systems, so that phone and e-mail of customer service reps can be scheduled on one master schedule. Others have Web-based systems that individual service reps can access to download their schedules, chart their productivity, or request time off without leaving their work stations.

Some features and functions are sold as add-on modules, which can increase your total investment, so it's important to clarify with the vendor what's included in the base package. Many vendors will tell you – and we agree – that it's a good idea to start with the base package and master it completely before adding more advanced modules such as schedule adherence scorecards.

Nor should you assume that all basic packages are created equal. We advise our clients to start by asking about a system's basic capabilities, features, and functions.

System requirements. Most scheduling software packages run on Windows or Windows NT platforms, and in most cases, you buy a standalone server that will network with your ACD. The packages that we have listed in the accompanying box are all interfaced with all of the major telephone switch makers. If appropriate, you'll also want to ask if the system supports multiple or mixed ACD environments and/ or multiple time zones.

Service rep scheduling variables. You'll want to ask how precisely you can program your schedule. How much information can it digest about your customer service representatives? How many fields of information can each service rep's individual file accommodate? Does it define work rules for employees, allowing for seniority or productivity? Are there interactive scheduling functions that service reps can access from their desks, enabling them to remain in their seats for their entire shift?

Overall call center variables. It's important to ascertain which variables about the overall call center operation the system takes into account and how flexible it is. Can it schedule for multiple and simultaneous events that take place throughout the seasons? What about multiple queues or skills? Does it allow you to specify varied service levels for different queues, times of day, days of the week, or teams and/ or catalogs? Does it factor in service levels like average speed of answer, acceptable abandonment rate, minimum/maximum calls handled?

Management functions. How can the scheduling package help you with key management decisions? Can it create "what-if" scenarios for budgeting or planning? Can it schedule for meetings and training? Can it tell you when you need to hire more staff and what skills and availability you'll need to look for? Does it analyze the effects of suggested hiring on your budget? Does it include a real-time or batch adherence function (or offer an add-on module) so that you can track absenteeism and tardiness?

Reports, analyses. Does the system print out individual service reps' schedules easily? Does it have robust and graphical reporting for management functions? Can it generate graphs to help service reps track their own productivity and attendance and compare themselves to the overall call center?

Installation, training, and support. How long will it take to set up the system and go live? How much training will your people need? Will training take place on your premises or off-site? How much ongoing technical support can you count on? Remember that you will likely need support not only for your staff, but also for the interface between the scheduling software and your telephone switch.

E-mail and Internet functions. Does the system interface with e-mail or chat management software so that you can centralize scheduling for reps who handle phone, Internet, or both? Is it accessible on the Web, so that reps can download their schedules from home or from their seats during their shift? Does the Web access enable supervisors to perform scheduling functions by logging on from wherever they are? Does it allow individual reps to communicate directly with their supervisors via e-mail – or with their peers to swap days or schedules? Call center scheduling is a complicated and potentially costly proposition, but the right scheduling software package can save both time and money and make your operation more efficient. Software developers in this field are continuing to come up with ingenious features and functions that will leave you more time for management duties and make you a better scheduler.

Determine Your IT Spend
Industry benchmarks can help you determine if your catalog is investing enough in information technology

By Paul Sobota

When it comes to information technology, what are catalog companies spending and why? On average, IT costs typically represent 1.80 to 2.2 percent of net sales for catalogs, according to new industry benchmarks revealed by F. Curtis Barry & Company.

These data provide a good base to measure your IT expenses against – in terms of efficiency, application development and technology. For example, you can determine:

1. Where do you need to go systems-wise, with what intensity and at what cost?
2. Are you meeting or exceeding the company's IT expectations? Does top management of your catalog, including the CEO and the CFO, know whether they are getting their money's worth for the investments they are making in IT systems?
3. What's your mode of operation? Are you interested in maintaining the status quo or your operations, or are you in an aggressive growth mode and looking for IT improvements?

Answering these questions can give you an idea of where you should be making your next IT investment.

F. Curtis Barry & Company's Information Technology ShareGroup studies show that IT departments in 22 catalogs with combined sales of $5.4 billion revealed that these catalogs had a total 47 million orders with combined IT expenses of $97 million. The expenses were compared on a blind basis between companies for major expense categories, including management, labor, hardware/software, services, telecom and facilities, among others.

The overall results of the 2003 F. Curtis Barry & Co. benchmarking study were as follows:

Total IT Costs as % Net Sales (in millions)			
By Sales Range	$5-$50 mill Net Sales	$51-$125 mill Net Sales	>$150 mill Net Sales
# of Companies	9	4	9
% Net Sales Range	0.78% - 4.84%	0.84% - 3.04%	0.94% - 3.39%
Avg. % Net Sales	2.19%	1.84%	1.79%

The figures do not include Internet IT expenses, which can vary widely depending on whether a catalog includes Web marketing as well as other 'Internet IT costs in the total. In this study, Internet IT costs ranged from 0.1 percent to 0.88 percent of net sales, and were excluded from the IT totals for ease of comparison. We also excluded telephone systems depreciation costs if they were included in the IT budget.

In looking at IT cost averages, be careful about how you view comparisons to net sales. Smaller catalog firms tended to have a higher fixed cost in proportion to provide comparable functions. While the largest budget belonged to a $1.4 billion cataloger who reports spending close to $30 million on IT, or a total of 1.99 percent of its net sales, interestingly, the most aggressive IT spending in terms of percent of sales came from companies of all sizes—not just the biggest catalogers.

Also, the smaller ($50 million and under) catalogers in the group had the greatest discrepancy in overall IT spending levels—a range from less than a percent to close to 5 percent. This perhaps demonstrates that some smaller catalogers are, on a percentage-basis, spending more currently due to ramping up their IT departments while other smaller catalogers may be marginally investing in IT systems.

Where's Your Money Going?

A careful review of your own IT expenses against this study of catalog industry IT benchmarks gives you a unique ability to get behind the numbers. By first defining your own company's IT expenses and then comparing notes, you can see where you stack up among other similar catalog companies in the business.

IT Cost Breakdown by Category (% to total IT costs-weighted average)	
Labor (includes benefits)	50.37%
- programming	(28.35%)
- ops/tech support	(17.17%)
- other	(4.85%)
Hardware	13.22%
Software	10.10%
Services	4.90%
Telecom	3.90%
Facilities	2.76%
Supplies	2.42%
Training	1.07%
Archived Storage	0.69%
Travel	0.69%
Other Costs	19.33%

For example, it's very important to realize that 50 percent of IT costs are labor (including programming, operations and tech support). Of course, committing to IT as part of your competitive strategy requires the staff to back it up. Small- to mid-sized catalogs, with sales in the $5 million to $50 million range averaged only 5 full-time employees, or the equivalent thereof. But the larger companies—those whose sales topped $150 million up to over $1 billion in sales, had the equivalent of between 21 full-time IT staff to 200-plus employees working in internal IT departments!

A related issue catalogers need to examine closely is in-house vs. outside systems development. More companies are developing at least some of their own IT systems in-house, according to our study, which showed 17 out of the 22 companies to be developers, with only five companies not developing their own IT (and even two of those five have their own programmers).

Whether it makes sense for your catalog operation to develop its own software and systems really depends on the complexity of your operations and what you're looking to the IT to accomplish for your business. Most often, we'll find catalogers using a combination of commercial systems in conjunction with proprietary, custom-developed applications. For catalogers that are non-developers, a key question to ask is, are commercial software vendors providing the needed functionality at a competitive price?

Regardless of whether you're looking at merely tweaking your current warehouse management system or an overhaul of your entire order management system, every catalog company should be actively engaged in IT planning. Requirements for successful IT planning include assessing what you have, what other industry leaders and competitors have, what you need now and your desires for the future. Only then can you effectively plan and budget for the development of in-house systems--or select and implement the appropriate commercial systems.

'Big Bang' Applications

When it comes to investing in information technology, catalog companies must determine their present mode of operation. In other words, when it comes to the technology to operate your business, consider whether you are:

1. In *maintenance mode*, merely looking to maintain current functionality;

2. In a *moderate growth mode*, seeking to add some new functionality and improvements to your systems; or In an *aggressive mode*, and ready to add some "big bang" applications to your IT capabilities.

3. If your company falls into the third category and you are serious about investing aggressively in IT, here are some areas where you may want to put your money:

Internet. For many catalogs today, the Internet represents about 20 to 30 percent of their direct sales. But for some catalogers, including six of the 22 we studied, the 'Net really grown in importance, representing from 40 percent to 70 percent of sales. Some areas worth investing in when it comes to Internet IT include:

1. Web order to business systems integration
2. Improved search engine optimization
3. Improved Web-based visibility across channels
4. Electronic gift certificates
5. Self service comparable to Customer Service
6. Web based systems

7. Predictive selling

Customer Contact Center. Whether on the phone or online, catalogers should be taking advantage of every customer contact to increase average order value, improve customer relations and maximize lifetime value.

1. Promotion upselling to increase average order size
2. Predictive selling software in the call center
3. Enhanced product data systems to decrease order time
4. CTI
5. Java, GUI and browser-based functions
6. Skill-based routing
7. CRM

Fulfillment/Supply Chain Management. In the warehouse, technology improvements can streamline business processes and improve accuracy and speed of order fulfillment.

1. PDA or Tablet PCs in QA and receiving
2. Web-based drop shipping
3. Best way, carrier rate shopping, new manifesting systems
4. Warehouse management system increase accuracy of inventory and reduced labor
5. UPC eliminates distribution ticketing and price change ticketing

Merchandising/Inventory Management. New systems for post season analysis, pre-season planning and in-season forecasting to improve fill rates, increase turnover and reduce backorders.

1. Integrated systems for marketing and merchandising
2. Age of inventory reporting track over stocks closer

Marketing/Creative. There is likely a wealth of actionable information about your customers in your database; the key is having the right systems to unleash it.

1. Data mining to find upsells/cross-sell relationships
2. In-house list processing
3. Electronic building of square inch
4. Eliminate duplicate names
5. E-mail marketing and affiliate marketing
6. Synergy between channels
7. Content management (digital assets)

Finance. The latest analytical processing tools can provide your catalog's executive management with the most up-to-date information about operations.

1. OLAP tools
2. Forecasting cash flow and centralized budgeting

How To Select Any Business System
Four Steps to Take Now

By Brian Barry

Whether your company is in need of a commercially packaged warehouse management system, point of sales system, inventory control system, direct-to-customer order management system – or some combination of the aforementioned, the selection of the right system is a major undertaking for your business. No matter what type of new system you're considering, that purchase is going to be a long-term investment. It has significant ramifications for how you serve your customers, the productivity of your personnel, and the management information it can provide to help you grow your business.

To make an accurate system assessment and choose the right system for your company's needs, we recommend you follow a four-step selection plan. This plan includes:

1. Organizing the project;
2. Defining your business needs;
3. Gaining a complete understanding of vendor's system and capabilities; and
4. Examining the expected ROI of the system.

By following these four steps, you can be assured of making a sound decision regarding the new system you select for your business.

Step 1: Organize the Project Internally

Before you begin reviewing systems, get the project organized within your company. For starters, you may want to appoint a management sponsor—someone in top management, such as a vice president of operations, who will represent the interests of the system's users. This will help elevate the project in terms of perceived importance, and encourage middle management and user departments to participate in the selection process.

It's also the time to set up a project steering committee, comprised of representatives from all areas that will be affected by the new system. Early on, the steering committee will identify the business functions to be accomplished by the new system. To assist the committee, management should provide the company's growth plans (three to five years) and any other anticipated changes in the business's direction. These include other channels of distribution, new catalogs, additional warehouses, changes in merchandise mix, etc. To further guide the selection process, management also should provide budget guidelines and decide whether the new system should run on existing hardware.

The steering committee will draw up a written plan for evaluating and selecting a vendor, and installing the system. It should then meet at least monthly to review the plan and the progress to date. A project coordinator can help keep the project on schedule and within budget.

Step 2: Define Your Requirements

Deciding what system functions you want is difficult. But keep in mind that this is critical in order to pick the right "match" for your needs. From our experience, the most effective systems generally have a 70 percent to 80 percent fit before modification. More extensive customizations lead to rewriting the system, which is generally expensive, risky, and delays implementation. It's a good idea to prioritize your functional requirements and divide them by each subsystem (e.g., order-entry, inventory or marketing). Include any unique requirements, key data elements missing from the current system, major screens and reports, and/or data interfaces to other systems.

Here's where a decision matrix approach can help. A decision matrix can be useful to evaluate a system's specific functions that you are requiring. It's a handy way to make quick comparisons between system vendors. The following is a sample decision matrix:

System evaluation matrix

This chart illustrates the use of a decision matrix to compare several vendors' inventory system functions. This analysis should be done for all system functions.

Rating methodology:

Priority legend: Must = Absolutely required - 3 points
                    Future = Need but not at once - 2 points
                    Nice = Would be beneficial, not required now - 1 point

Vendor responses: Yes = Has/acceptable as is - 4 points
                    Yes-mod = Has modification to meet requirements - 3 points
                    No-mod = Does not have but will provide - 2 points
                    No = Does not have and will not provide - 1 point

Rating Computation: Multiply Priority points by vendor response points for each Function.

Example: Priority "Must" (3 pts.) X response "Yes" (4 pts.) = 12 pts.

Report Functions

Priority	Function	Vendor 1 Response/rating	Vendor 2 Response/rating
Future	One screen/report to make rebuy decisions	Yes-mod...6	Yes-mod...6
Must	Can calculate units required for life-of-catalog	No-mod...6	Yes...12
Must	Data presented in units	Yes...12	Yes...12
Nice	Data presented in $s	No-mod...2	Yes-mod...3
Must	Report data for items in multiple catalogs	Yes...12	No-mod...6
Must	Ability to enter percents for:		
	1. Order completion	No-mod...6	Yes...12
	2. Returns	No-mod...6	Yes-mod...9
	3. Cancellations	No-mod...6	Yes-mod...9
	By catalog, category or item		
Must	Detail audit trail or inventory transactions	Yes...12	Yes...12
Must	Can inventory data be summarized and reported with totals by color, item category and catalog	No-mod...6	Yes...12
		Point Total: 74	Point Total: 93

Comments about evaluation matrix:

This catalog company features women's apparel, shoes and some gifts. Some of the items are reorderable. Vendor 1 presently has no installed apparel users. The vendor's orientation is more business-to-business, and there are separate demand, sales and inventory statistics by catalog. The six "no-mod" responses indicate a more severe level of change would be needed for Vendor 1's system to meet the catalog's requirements when compared to Vendor 2. In contrast, Vendor 2's system is designed for and has been implemented for apparel and shoe catalog merchandise. Consequently, it has a better "fit" to the requirements. In both cases, however, all modifications should be cost estimated.

Step 3: Evaluate the Vendors

In your request for proposal (RFP), make sure you specify that bidders include in writing all of the pricing, guarantees and schedules for the application; the software and hardware to be provided; pre-installation training; modifications required before and after installation; a list of other package systems that have been successfully integrated with; and file conversion and support.

Scripted demonstrations. Now comes the tough part: comparing multiple vendors and their system's features and functions. Use the RFP responses and scripted demos to work through which system has a better fit for your company. Many companies don't allow enough time for a complete demo. Often a full two days is needed to review all of the functionality of a complex commercial system. A scripted demo will help you target the functions most important to your business and any potential modifications required. It will require vendors to show functions that you want to see during the demo rather than the functions that the vendor wants to show you.

Reference checks and site visits. It is imperative to check vendor references. Don't just rely on the list that the vendor supplies to you. Get the entire list of users, and go beyond the requested list of references. Find out as much as you can about the vendor from its users. You should come up with a scripted list of questions for the reference checks. The questions should discuss things like features used and system support. This scripting is done so that you have asked the same questions of each reference check and can make comparisons between them later. Just as important as the reference checks is taking scheduled trips to system users that are similar to your business (e.g., apparel, hardgoods, wholesale, etc.). When making these user site visits, make these trips without the vendor present. This allows the users to be as open and frank about the system as possible.

Vendor support. As you are selecting and evaluating a system package, find out how well the vendor will continue to update and enhance the system and support the system in the future. That is the reason why you are buying a commercial system. Does the vendor have a schedule for new releases with new functions, and what is the frequency? Do most enhancements/modifications for individual clients get added into the future enhancements and releases of the system? Also you need to find out how timely are responses with regard to software bugs and problems. What is the size of the vendor's support team, and is it a full-time team dedicated to supporting the system and its users?

The age of the system and the system design will determine how well the vendor can support you in the long term. If the system is more than five years old, it has probably been modified extensively. How easy will it be to get the modifications you are requesting, and at what cost? Determine these changes in advance of signing the con-tract. Will the system give you a good base to grow your business? The age of the system may also determine how innovative and user-friendly it is; for example, is it character-based or Windows-based?

During the implementation phase, vendor support will be important in thoroughly testing any modifications you need on the base package. Since running existing and new systems in parallel is usually not affordable for most companies from a time or cost perspective, a full systems test should be accomplished by all users, assuring readiness for implementation.

Finally, as part of the selection process, review the vendors' approach to training and file conversion. Which files will be converted? How will these be converted, and by whom?

Step 4: Examine the System's Potential ROI

Wouldn't it be great to be able to measure the return on investment (ROI) of a new business system purchase before you make that major investment? Well, you can – if you take the time to examine all the costs involved in the purchase along with the specific returns you expect to gain from implementing the new system.

Don't fall into the trap of basing your ROI calculation on the vendor's canned promotion data – however well intentioned it may be. You need to take the time to run these numbers yourself. In order to get the most accurate sense of your potential ROI upfront, do the following calculation: Divide the total cost of the system investment by the average annual improvement you hope to gain. The result of this calculation will be the number of years it will take to recoup the investment. In that time period, the gains you will have made will equal your initial investment. Any gains thereafter can be considered true ROI. For a more precise application of this formula, apply the savings on a monthly calendar until you have zeroed out the investment, especially if you have a seasonal business as many consumer catalogers and multi-channel marketers do.

Be Thorough

Having completed the four-step selection process, by now you should have gathered enough information to make a good purchase decision. But don't rush into anything: Remember, selecting a new system involves many factors, so conduct a thorough search and allow enough time for each step in the process. A full understanding of your needs and the vendor's capabilities should ultimately result in a successful installation.

How Your Company Can Ensure Smooth System Selection And Implementation

By Paul Sobota

Systems selection and implementation is serious business, and no one wants to make an already complex process more difficult or more costly. Over the years, F. Curtis Barry & Company has determined some principles to follow during an implementation project that will significantly improve the chances of success for all parties concerned. There may not be any absolute guarantees, but following these ten proven principles will definitely smooth the way for your next implementation project.

1. Adhere to a well-disciplined, proven methodology for selection and implementation.

2. Have executive management buy in and sign off at various points. We have learned that if we do not document the decisions and progress of the project and report on a regular basis to executive management, business decisions and changes in the scope of the original project may conflict with what management has in mind. Consistent, objective status reporting may bring to light issues that the vendor or the project team may have neglected to bring to the attention of management.

3. Perform thorough and proper due diligence to ensure a close fit

between your business requirements and the application you have selected. Be sure to include a low number of modifications and clearly define interfaces and data conversion issues.

4. When you discover serious discrepancies, it's better to change the business process to fit the system, where realistic, rather than modify the system heavily. Modifications result in higher costs, risks, and potential delay of the implementation. We have learned that, unlike e-commerce software models, a so-called fully customizable solution is not necessarily the best fit for many businesses.

We used to advocate modifying applications to be more in line with the business, but it is better to make sure that the system's business process can really be adopted by the business. We learned that modifications and complex integrations are risky and expensive and can cause serious delays. Often modifications turn out to be unnecessary once the new system is fully understood by the new users.

5. Demand that the internal project manager and the vendor project manager be well disciplined and organized. We have learned that we need to help support our client company with these tasks. There have been instances where a project has suffered because the client's project manager was not well organized or capable of multi-tasking and keeping the project team up to date.

6. Select a DTC system that can support features and functions in the intended marketplace (appropriate sales channels, application integrations, SKU numbering, etc).

7. Adhere to a well-defined project plan and timeline that suits both vendor and client, making sure to a lot sufficient time for each

task without jeopardizing the project. Appropriate status reporting is crucial for monitoring the overall progress of each task.

8. Make sure you have a fair and well-defined, detailed negotiated contract including statement of work, pricing for hardware, software licenses, modifications, training, file conversion, etc.

9. Require budget approval of estimates and of any change in scope prior to the work performed.

10. Although difficult to quantify, good chemistry between client, vendors, and consultants is important to the success of systems selection and implementation.

Systems Development Considerations: Build vs. Buy?

By Paul Sobota

Whether you're in need of new fulfillment software or a system for your call center, you'll likely have a choice to make between a packaged software system and custom-created solutions that you develop in-house, with or without expert help.

What determines whether to purchase packaged software or to pursue developing systems internally?

Both possible avenues start with the same information-gathering processes:

- Form a project team from the applicable departments the system(s) will affect, including a member from top management; this person will act as the project sponsor.

- Appoint a steering committee to meet and review the project on a periodic basis.

- Formulate an RFP from the requirements determined by the members of the project team.

- Develop costs for internal development from the same

requirements.

- Determine the percent fit from the RFP responses.

- Compare vendor costs to in-house development costs to reach your conclusion.

In some instances, packaged software may be just the solution your company needs. But large companies looking to move away from legacy systems often find that packaged software doesn't meet 80 percent of their requirements, as they may have developed many unique features to support their business requirements.

What happens when the vendor responses don't meet at least 80 percent of your requirements? Then, modifications are needed to the vendor's package. It is important to recognize that modifications equal additional costs and risks, extended timeframes to implement, additional testing, documenting and training, etc. When this occurs, the cost of the off-the-shelf, packaged software solution is likely to increase, so take this possibility into account when making your cost comparison.

Why doesn't the user community of the packaged software vendors push to have more functionality?

- Vendors may have limited development staff.

- Vendors may not have the depth of experience to understand the new functionality and need assistance from their user community.

- Time and cost to develop may exceed what the vendor is willing to commit to.

When packaged software vendors can't meet your company's needs the alternative is to continue to develop in-house. This presents a different set of opportunities and challenges:

- Internal development and maintenance costs and time frames can be difficult to project.

- Is the legacy system written in an outdated language?

- Does your staff have broad enough industry knowledge to know best practices? Are there development personnel who understand the current system processes and the new requirements in order to effectively develop the modifications?

- Documentation (both system and user) is usually put off until after the modifications are completed and then may not get done as the analysts and programmers are off on the next assignment. Without documentation any modification becomes difficult to maintain especially when the original designer/developer is no longer employed at the company.

An added challenge to developing your own software is it doesn't allow you to take advantage of the input from the vendors' user committee, who, hopefully, is guiding the direction of new functionality. Advice from other users can be very enlightening in deciding where to take the software to the next levels.

Decision Time

In the end you will need to develop a game plan that works best for your company whether you are developing your own systems or selecting and installing packaged software.

Warehouse Management Systems: Are They Right For Catalogers And For You?

By Bob Betke

Cataloging in the United States has reached a level of maturity that places it on equal footing with other channels of communication and distribution. No longer dominated by entrepreneurs and small to medium-sized companies whose primary concern was just scrambling to get orders out the door in a timely fashion, catalogs – and catalog fulfillment – mean big business.

Catalog businesses are consolidating at an unprecedented rate. New players — manufacturers, department and specialty stores electronic retailers, multi-site distributors, and others — are entering the field, often bringing with them highly sophisticated logistics experience. At the same time, catalog customers are demanding—and getting from larger companies — same day pick and ship in business-to-business or, in some consumer catalogs, a 24-hour turnaround, with a high degree of probability that the items they order will be in stock.

With competition more fierce than ever, management is looking at fulfillment, to gain a marketing advantage in terms of increased efficiency and improved customer service.

Faced with these challenges, more and more catalog companies, particularly in the mid-sized range, are investigating warehouse management systems (WMS), both to improve operations and to provide a higher level of sophistication and control in fulfillment than catalog management software (CMS) typically provides.

This first in a series of articles looks at the benefits of warehouse management systems and examines their worth in terms of productivity and accuracy. In subsequent articles, we will review individual WMS vendors and their systems.

Are you a WMS candidate?

Annual sales, number of orders and returns processed, number of units shipped, type and value of product—all may impact whether or not the investment in a warehouse management system is right for your company. But, if you have ever asked yourself any of the following questions or faced any of the following situations, the degree of functionality or flexibility found in even the most basic WMS may be just what you need to bring your company into the 21st century:

- "Even with all of the care we take to check and double check work, too many mistakes in order picking are still happening. What's the solution?"

- "We don't seem to have enough space to operate efficiently anymore. But this doesn't make sense because I know that this warehouse should hold more."

- "Why can't we find merchandise where it's supposed to be"?

- "When volume goes up, you'd expect costs to come down. Now that we're bigger, why aren't we experiencing any economies of scale"?

WMS—a definition

Simply stated, a warehouse management system is a method of managing and tracking all activity of product and people through all warehouse functions using bar code and radio frequency (RF) technology to gather and communicate information. A WMS controls all activity in receiving, quality control, putaway, replenishment, pick/pack/ship, manifest, returns, physical inventory, and labor and productivity measurement reporting.

A wide range of companies are currently investing in WMS projects, including:

- A department store that has established a fast-growing direct-marketing catalog;

- A luxury goods retailer/direct marketer that has outgrown its homegrown warehousing system;

- A consumer products manufacturer that has entered direct marketing through the Internet with first year sales of $50 million going direct to the consumer;

- A home decor retailer/cataloger with multiple distribution centers, serving both channels;

- A business-to-business cataloger with multiple distribution centers;

- A traditional catalog company whose recent rapid growth has resulted in severe inventory shrinkage and also large inventory write-downs.

For these companies—looking for more timely and more accurate inventory control—current CMS systems no longer meet their needs.

Most catalog management systems are geared to meet the complex requirements of the front end of the business—customer service, order entry, in season forecasting, and marketing. And the greatest demand for improving these systems comes from the front-end-- marketing, merchandising, and inventory forecasting.

Although all of these systems have warehouse functionality, they do not provide the level of sophistication and depth found in most standard warehouse management systems. Conceptually, as enterprise software, catalog management systems typically coordinate an entire company's business requirements and support the information-system needs across all departments, from marketing to accounting, merchandising to order taking. As such, they attempt to fully integrate information in that they share data among functions and share a common database, but they generally provide only elementary capabilities when it comes to complicated transportation and warehousing tasks for moderate to large catalogs.

Catalog management systems, for example, are not able to handle the complex logistics or optimization routines that are often involved, for example, in analyzing truck routings among several distribution sites or inventory handling in real time within a warehouse. WMS, in contrast, focus on specific logistics tasks and, therefore, provide the kind of depth that is needed to drive specific functions as well as realize real productivity gains in each function.

To illustrate the difference, there are some major sub-systems that catalog management systems cannot provide at all or as fully developed functional features. Some of these sub-systems have been created piecemeal as catalogers have demanded them. One CMS vendor,

for example, has just added the ability to track multiple warehouses
when its largest user has had four warehouses for many years.

In addition, most catalog management systems lack productivity
measurement, reporting by department function, full integration of
bar-code tracking from dock receiving through inventory movement,
pick verification, inventory cycle counts, bulk-to-forward inventory
replenishment, advanced kitting and de-kitting capabilities, as well as
QC specification and reporting. They also are unable to generate bar-
code pallet, license plate and carton labels.

Some drawbacks

As a specialized or best-of-breed system, warehouse management
software augments a company's current catalog management system. The result is that, instead of dealing with one vendor and a single set of numbers, catalogers installing WMS now must deal with
two different vendors, two different support staffs, as well as the integration of the system with other systems in the company (interfaces to
retail, registry, accounting, as well as the CMS). That, in turn, means
increased costs, which need to be justified against the long-term gains
in productivity and accuracy.

The most critical interface, without question, is the interface to the
catalog management system. The information required to operate the
WMS must be transferred back and forth between the WMS and the
CMS. Crucial to successful integration is the design phase of the overall system so that both systems operate effectively. Also, there are
additional costs for some customization or other modifications to the
WMS system in order to perform special consumer, small order, pick/
pack/ship because not all catalog, retail, or manufacturing companies
have the same characteristics or need the same special services (for
example, gift wrap, personalization, and so forth).

In spite of these drawbacks, a warehouse management system provides a compelling solution for catalogers who are trying to increase customer service and reduce costs by:

- Reducing the labor cost per unit handled,

- Reducing the amount of space needed to store each unit,

- Reducing the frequency of errors, and

- Improving measurement and overall performance.

These improvements are the result of the enormous impact a WMS can have on each function in a warehouse operation. The following list, though not all inclusive, outlines WMS functions by operational area:

Receiving

A WMS provides management with quicker access to updated information about product status. At receiving, a WMS may initiate the paperless warehouse through the scanning of purchase orders and products. The receiving process starts at the dock, logging in the carrier, the number of cartons or pallets received, any visible damage, the purchase order number on the side of the carton, the vendor identification. From the minute, merchandise hits the dock, warehouse management systems generates license plates and carton labels. Typically, purchase order writing remains in the CMS application.

Future possible applications will include the use of advance shipping notices (ASN) to generate an updated receiving document (not based on outdated, original PO information). Applications with EDI are also currently being created.

Inspection/QC

The specifications and standards that your company inspects against can be included. Reports indicating the results of the inspection can also be generated. After merchandise is opened and inspected, WMS can direct merchandise to appropriate bin/slot locations, reserve storage, cross docking, or to further holding for disposition. Bar codes are used to track merchandise throughout this process.

Putaway

License plate or case bar-code labels and bar-coded warehouse locations may be used to confirm that the correct merchandise is in the proper location. This results in a positive record of location for future use and tracking, which may also be used for increased cube utilization in the warehouse as well as reduced travel time through directed putaway. Although both operator-directed and system-directed putaway are available in most warehouse management systems, the most common used is operator-directed.

Replenishment

The ability to have product in the primary pick slot when it is needed is one of the keys to successful fulfillment. With WMS, quicker and more accurate restocking of primary pick slots result. Finding and verifying the correct location and product can be accomplished with reduced searching time and increased accuracy. Replenishment can be directed by the WMS system or manually driven. All applications can use portable, hand-held scanning units or fixed work stations.
Because of the increased ability to find merchandise, it may be possible to reduce your inventory level to some extent by lowering the amount of safety stock you normally keep on hand, although this is not necessarily true for all operations.

Picking

With the use of bar-code and RF systems, catalogers are able to verify 100% of the picks that take place, if desired. With real-time verification of the proper locations of merchandise, immediate corrections, if necessary can be completed, thus reducing errors. The lower the level of barcoding that is done in the warehouse, the higher the percentage of accuracy. With WMS, having bar codes attached at the unit level, rather than the case level, results in improved accuracy. Because each business has different requirements, it is imperative that a cost analysis be undertaken, to determine the incremental savings to be realized versus the added time and expense required to detail information at the unit level.

WMS provides the flexibility to match the picking methods with order profile and warehouse layout as your business changes. Multiple methods of generating pick tickets may also be created or paperless picking employed, if desired. Multiple methods of generating pick tickets also maximize operating efficiency in that they can be made to match the actual orders received--for example, someone with a high percentage of single line orders would probably use a batch picking method, whereas someone with a number of multi-line orders might consider cart/bin picking. The more sophisticated or automated warehouses usually employ wave picking.

Packing

Picking accuracy may be checked or re-checking by scanning orders and actual units selected at the packing station. Scanning for diverting and sortation to pack stations and shipping lanes is also possible in more automated warehouses. If the picker picks into the final shipping container using bar-coded verification, subsequent checking may be eliminated and packing expedited. "Clean" packing documents--or documents that reflect actual products shipped--and invoices may also be produced.

Manifesting, Shipping/Tracking

Although the first use of bar codes in most catalog operations occurred in the manifest area, future enhancements in WMS are expected to come in the form of data integration with your catalog management system. Now, with WMS and CMS, carrier tracking systems are accessible for customer service inquiries, as well as to the existing tracking systems.

Returns

Bar codes on returns and their paperwork speed processing, increase accuracy, return merchandise to stock as available inventory more quickly, and channel product for other disposition more efficiently. Coding of return reasons and product condition is possible, as is faster crediting of customer accounts. De-picking functions speed the return to stock, thus making it more readily available for future picking. The precise detailing of information, in addition to being accessed immediately, results in better customer service.

Inventory Control

Another major benefit of WMS is the ability to know exactly where stock is and how much stock is available at all times. It also allows you to identify available empty bins and slots. All of this results in increased space utilization because stock can be re-located and consolidated quickly. Tracking of product by move and operator helps measure productivity and accountability while reducing inventory mistakes and shrinkage. Stock rotation and the ability to react to date-sensitive stock and other special storage requirements are also accommodated.

Physical Inventory/Cycle Counting

With bar codes, it is possible to interleave counting with such other functions as putaway, replenishment, or picking. Physical cycle counts, when required, are expedited by having less paperwork and accurate locations. Studies have shown that inventory accuracy with WMS can approach 100%. Eliminating annual or semi-annual physical counting is possible. Counting critical items--fast sellers or high-value products--on a cyclical basis is achievable because locations and counts per location are available. That means one product located in many different areas can be counted accurately. Without the real-time tracking of WMS, you may know the total amount of product you have, but you may not know how much product is in each location at any given time. Inventory shrinkage of 0.5% or lower is commonplace.

Productivity Tracking and Reporting

The tracking of work performed by individual and the time required to complete each task generally lead to productivity increases. With WMS, catalogers are able to measure time spent on indirect activites-- waiting, cleaning and maintainence, or other functions, for example-- as well as on direct functions--picking/packing, receiving, putaway, and shipping. The true measurement of labor costs by function also improves the quality of future decisions about proposed changes in operations. As a general rule, overall productivity gains far exceed the extra time required to use the RF bar-coded equipment that measures each work task.

Specialized Functions

Catalogs with special product requirements--product personalization and/or customization, special sizing, assembly, or production considerations--find it difficult to track, monitor, locate, and report the status of these products. WMS gives catalogers improved accuracy and control.

Kitting/De-Kitting

Many operations require the ability to instruct and track both kitting and de-kitting activities, which is probably one of the most difficult tasks to perform in a warehouse. As a complex function involving everything from order entry through shipping, kitting/de-kitting is not handled well in most catalog management systems. WMS, on the other hand, provides a means to do this efficiently.

Justification of investment

At present, the above operational functions may be found in almost every basic warehouse management system, without special modifications or programming. The kind of expanded functionality being asked for by many of today's catalog companies, however, is being driven by consumer demand, competition, and the increasing complexities of the catalog business itself. But even with these pressures, the investment in a new system that, additionally, must be integrated into the existing catalog management system requires cost-justification.

There are two main areas for savings—accuracy and productivity. Common to both is the generation and management of information in a timely manner.

Critical to warehouse improvement is the use data to understand your operation—its inefficiencies and waste—in order to support decisions for change and increased efficiency. Another advantage of having data available company-wide is that, when information is shared— rather than isolated in the heads of a few key individuals—there is greater accountability. In addition, it ensures that the organization will operate routinely even if these individuals, for whatever reason, are no longer a part of your organization.

Because studies we have conducted show that the typical backorder costs between $7 and $12 to process, inventory accuracy to help reduce backorders is also critical.

Accuracy is particularly important since an error in the warehouse that results in a mis-shipment can cost between $20 and $50. To determine the true cost of an error, the following cost factors need to be evaluated:

- Customer service call
- Average of one follow-up call
- Picking, packing and shipping the correct item
- Processing the returned item, including restocking where possible.
- Reshipping charge for the correct item
- Overhead charge @ 20%
- Customer dissatisfaction in the long term
- Cancellation of the order rather than an exchange.

Improved productivity is another major selling point of a WMS. Of course, the percentage productivity increases you can realize depends on your present operations and systems, as well as on the extent to which you are already using bar codes.

Although catalogers tend to justify spending money on bar codes through increased productivity, most savings actually come from improvements in accuracy and material control. However, even if the accuracy and productivity savings prove to be relatively minor, they should be investigated further to determine if the WMS will result in basic alteration of operational methods, which may create a previously unanticipated return on investment.

Reduction in walk time (often 70% to 80% of pickers' time), checking, paperwork, search time, error correction and physical inventories can easily occur with the information and control bar coding provides. These opportunistic savings should also be factored into your calculations.

In addition to measurable cost-savings potential, there are indirect benefits that also may be attributed to improved accuracy and productivity. Among the savings are the following:

- Reduced stock outs
- Reduced backorders
- Lower inventory, possibly reduced safety stock
- Increased space utilization; increased inventory turns
- Ability to measure you entire operation
- Increases in the life-time value of a satisfied customer, and
- Enhanced corporate image and marketing potential.

The selection process

After the decision is made to proceed with the implementation of a WMS, the difficult task of vendor evaluation begins. The first step is to narrow down the potential list of vendors. This can be a daunting task in itself because there are several hundred vendors who claim to sell some WMS functionality in their products. (The chart that accompanies this article represents a sampling of WMS vendors from small to large companies with systems that work on different types of platforms. These vendors are provided as a starting point for vendor evaluation. No endorsement of them is implied).

After speaking to a wide variety of vendors about your basic needs, your initial sort should result in a list of about ten vendors.

Next, you need to prepare a request for proposal (RFP). It should include a prioritized list of functional requirements, expected transaction volumes, and any other special conditions that you need. Try to frame as many of the questions you have so that you can delineate your requirements in terms that will result in quantifiable information in the returned RFP. This effort will facilitate comparisons among vendors' RFP's later. A weighting of each factor will aid this process. Each requirement is weighted both by the user's priority for it and the vendor's ability to provide it. Also, detailed information from those vendor's who will receive your RFP should be requested and added to their files. This information should include number of installations, number of employees, type of platforms their system runs on, and so forth.

Crucial to the entire requirements or needs assessment process is the involvement of all levels of the warehouse, not just top management. Be sure to ask for input of the people who really understand how things work in the warehouse and seek out the comments of the front-line warehouse employees who are picking and packing every day.

The actual selection should take into account the following: response to the requirements in the RFP, the cost of the system, answers to questions about the vendor organization, site visits, software demonstrations, and reference checks. Finding a vendor who has experience with your type of business is, obviously a real plus.

In all likelihood, there will be some degree of modifications or customization required with the system. This fine-tuning needs to be considered when evaluating cost, as well as when implementing a schedule and time line.

Systems costs range from $100,000 to several million dollars. The total investment should be in the area of $200,000 to $500,000 for a basic system in a warehouse of 100,000 square feet. When approached by us to find a way to reduce this outlay for the smaller cataloger and still provide basic, off-the-shelf functionality, a number of vendors we contacted indicated interest.

As a general rule, it is important not to over design the system or develop a wish list of requirements that add only marginal benefits to your operations. It is far better to stick to fulfillment basics and to use WMS as a tool to help you to achieve those basics.

If your operation is currently operating with a high degree of sophistication, then you are ready to use WMS to move you and your company to the next level. If, on the other hand, you are, for example, not using slot numbers in your operation, then do not try to make the leap in technology to provide that kind of capability. It can cause your program to fail. It is better to take improvements in steps, to ensure a successful implementation, even though it may on the surface seem like a good time to re-engineer the entire warehouse. Such an aggressive undertaking should be approached carefully.

A final word

Although catalogers are beginning to express interest in WMS, there are only a few vendors who have installed their systems in catalog companies and those installations are in some of the largest catalogs. Given growth in the catalog business, however, it's only a matter of time until systems will be developed to meet the cataloger's special interests.

Moreover, there is also an opportunity for CMS software vendors to team up with WMS vendors and fine tune their programs. An alliance such as this would reduce the high level of investment CMS vendors would need to make in program development, as well as make their products more attractive to larger prospective catalog companies that may now view current catalog management systems as inadequate to meet their needs.

[Note: Mr. Barry does not endorse any direct marketing software packages, and he urges readers to use these reviews only as a starting point for acquiring or rejecting a warehouse management system].

Warehouse & Distribution

Conducting A Post Season Audit On Your Fulfillment Operations, Part I

By Bob Betke

Although the 2007 holiday season hasn't ended yet for many multichannel merchants, many of our clients are already preparing for holiday 2008. You should, too, by conducting a post-season audit. This process enables you to challenge your group to find ways to reduce costs and at the same time get critical data and observations to be used for the next holiday season.

In the first of this two-part series, we will cover the basics of performing a post-season audit as a base line for process improvement and cost reduction. Part II will discuss the major potential cost reduction areas of the distribution center.

The first step in the audit is to form a post-season review team, which should include fulfillment supervisors and some key personnel in the DC. The team's observations of what went right, what was marginal, and what needs to be fixed before next year should include finding answers to these questions:

- What was the labor cost per order shipped during the increased staffing period of your holiday season, vs. your balance-of-year average cost per order shipped? This identifies how effectively you used the temporary holiday labor and how it performed.

- What was the cost of training the seasonal labor force? Were they brought in at the right time for sufficient training and to match volume surges, or were they on the payroll too early?

- What was the found error rate and subsequent rework required? Are they higher than normal? Why did they increase?

- Did you use your experienced associates to pick and teach seasonal temps to pack? You should: It is easier and faster to teach packing than to teach picking, and if you use your experienced people to pick, your error rate should be lower.

- Did you cross-train all regular associates to pack during the course of the year? Were they available to fill in for peaks after performing such tasks as receiving, put away, administrative/ clerical, etc.? This enables you to hold down the number of seasonal temps required.

- What was the rate of overtime during the holiday season versus the balance of the year? Also calculate labor man-hours per order shipped during the holiday season vs. the balance-of-year average. Low wages paid to temps may drive down the cost per order, but man hours used will identify your true performance.

- What was the turnover rate for seasonal employees and for what reasons? How many rehires did you have to make, adding to training cost and putting inexperienced people to work? Too frequently, inexperienced and insufficiently trained people make little contribution and drive up costs.

- Were there any issues with shortages of supplies? Why?

- How did holiday volume perform to the sales forecast? A post-

season audit is critical to understanding DC management's re-
sponsiveness.

- How did the DC perform daily against order volume? Did the facility fall behind scheduled shipments? How far behind by day?
  What was the order carryover identified as both orders and a percent carryover by day?

- Did your carriers perform? Were their pickups on schedule?

- Were there any bottlenecks in the flow of work? Why did they
  occur and how can they be averted next year?

- What was your post-holiday season rate of returns? What were the
  reasons for returns, which were DC related (i.e. picking error, broken in transit, etc)? What was the turn around period between receiving the return and processing refund or exchanges? Any areas
  or bottlenecks in the returns process that need to be corrected?
  Was there sufficient receiving space? Did it infringe on outbound
  space?

To help answer these questions, use departmental reports throughout
the center. These include transaction volume reports for orders received, picked, shipped, manifested, returns, back orders processed;
service levels achieved (standard or plan and actual) payroll and productivity reports (budgeted and actual); DC inventory control reports
about inventory adjustments, products not found in picking process,
error reporting, etc.

Conducting A Post Season Audit On Your Fulfillment Operations, Part 2: Reducing Costs In The DC

By Bob Betke

With the peak volume of the holiday season over, you should have just about finished your post-season audit of your operation. As we discussed in the previous article, this will give you a good idea of how and where you can reduce and control expenses in your distribution center.

Now it's time to implement some changes. Where should you start? Here's a checklist of some steps to take.

- Bring your workforce down to the size required for your post-holiday business forecast. Nothing increases costs more than excess people on the payroll—and by attempting to manage hours with too large a staff, you'll wind up sending employees home early multiple days per week, running the risk of losing key associates who can't afford to work less than 40 hours.

  This is also a great time to evaluate all employees and retain the workers who performed best. Frequently you'll find gems in the seasonal staff who are better than some of your regular associates. So bite the bullet, make the difficult decisions, and reduce staff quickly.

- Perform inventory consolidation in your storage area, both to organize storage and create space for new product arrivals. Consolidating inventory now will save inbound labor dollars later, as well as ease and expedite the ability to locate product.

- Assure your key performance metrics are in place for pick, pack, ship, replenish, receive and put away. Be certain you are generating reporting on all the key indices which will help you manage expenses, including labor hours and dollars (regular and premium) measured against volumes received and shipped (units, lines, orders, boxes).

- Reconfigure your slotting and pick locations to reduce travel time to a minimum. Relocate items appropriately to slow moving or to fast moving picks to create efficiency. Remove seasonal items from the pick line so you are not walking by them each day.

- If you didn't cross-train all regular associates to pack last year, begin now for next year and continue cross-training throughout the year. Be sure any new employees retained from the seasonal worker ranks are fully trained and performing to standard. Training for seasonal associates is often quick, so if you are retaining people, make sure they are properly trained to be successful.

- Develop a fulfillment to-do list from your post-season audit. Assign responsibilities and follow up to assure the tasks are being performed.

- If you have never developed goals and objectives for your operation and your fulfillment staff, this is the perfect time to start. Goals and objectives or key performance indicators are the most objective method of evaluating individual performance. Successful accomplishment of goals and objectives adds to the profitability of the company.

- Create your fulfillment budget for the next fiscal year. Remember that an effective budget reflects improvement in performance and reduction of expense to enable the company to offer wage increases where appropriate.

- Review transportation contracts. When shipping volume is down, every penny of cost becomes critical. Knowledgeable review of both inbound and outbound transportation contracts and costs can typically yield savings up to 20%.

- Consult with your supply vendors for packaging, corrugated, Styrofoam, etc. Are you able to return overstock for credit? Again, every penny saved during slow periods is important.

- Determine if this is the time for experienced help to assist you in reconfiguring the warehouse. There are many ways to improve layout within your current walls to expand capacity and improve efficiency.

Along those lines, are your systems generating the necessary results in the required time periods, or is your fulfillment center losing efficiency because your systems are unable to perform? This is a great time to develop a systems requirement document identifying your needs for growth and for performance.

- Conduct objective individual performance evaluations for your salaried staff. Objective and honest evaluations of individual performance are the building blocks of great teams.

And finally, the only good thing about slow volume is that it affords you the opportunity to evaluate past performance failures and to implement change for future performance successes.

Trends, Best Practices And Metrics In Fulfillment

By Bob Betke

These are challenging times for the multichannel industry. On the basis of our consulting assignments in multichannel operations and fulfillment and proprietary data from the F. Curtis Barry & Company Benchmarking ShareGroups, we have identified several current trends in multichannel fulfillment, and ways in which businesses are addressing these trends by implementing industry best practices.

In the most positive light, challenges can also present opportunities in managing fulfillment. The challenges we see include: A need to increase productivity; dramatic increases in transportation costs; a continual rise in direct labor costs as well as in the availability and quality of the work force; compressed seasonal order peaks; higher customer expectations; more companies focusing on supply chain opportunities to decrease costs and increase customer service; competitors reducing costs and service times; and China import problems.

Reducing operations costs

The phrase "cost of operation" now encompasses the concept of maximizing return on all assets, including employees, facility, inventory, material handling equipment, and systems and software. The No. 1 issue for many direct operations is how to reduce the two largest costs—direct labor and inbound and outbound freight.

Acquisitions

In the past few years, venture capital and private equity firms have acquired an unprecedented number of major multichannel businesses. We see many multi-brand operations being merged and consolidated into a smaller number of larger call centers and fulfillment centers that process multiple titles or brands. These companies are continually looking at process improvements in order to stay competitive.

Multiple warehouse locations

As companies strive to deliver faster to the customer, keep their ability to supply stores within a day's transportation time, and decrease freight costs, many are considering multiple distribution centers. The downside of such a move includes the increased span of control necessary, increased inventory, and the need for fulfillment systems with inventory functions robust enough to manage multiple centers. In evaluating potential new locations, a business should look at these critical success factors: labor cost, quality, and availability; inbound and outbound freight costs; facility costs; and economic incentives.

Performance requirements and metrics

Improvement requires measurement, and fulfillment operations now recognize the need to capture metrics for regular and overtime man hours and labor dollars worked and paid, and then to develop comparisons to volume measurement as units, lines, or orders shipped (see sidebar, "Fulfillment Operations Metrics") for current direct fulfillment operations standards.

Labor cost, availability, and quality

Direct companies must frequently compete for workers with other warehouse operations. Pay rates in many markets have risen above $11.00 per hour, compared to $7.00 per hour just five years ago. In site location studies, we are finding that labor availability and quality compete with transportation costs as the most important factor in deciding to move a DC.

This increase in labor cost is often accompanied by a decrease in absolute productivity in terms of units of work output. Since direct labor is 50% or more of the fulfillment expense, companies must find ways to reverse this trend. The basis for improvement is to set expectations for performance (such as units per man hour for pick/pack), measure results, and provide feedback to employees and management.

Employee retention

Employee turnover is expensive. Employers need to tell employees what is expected and give them feedback, and to create a work culture that makes people want to stay. Most people want to know how they are doing and to be part of a team.

Staff development and communication

Many businesses are realizing that they need stronger first-line managers. Typical issues include how to get better production; motivating employees; getting first-line managers to help plan changes to accommodate order and inventory volume growth; managing a multilingual workforce; and managing a workforce with flex schedules. Is there a career path company-wide for potential managers?

Improving the capacity of existing facilities

Expanding or relocating a facility is expensive and places customer service at risk. The trend is to improve space utilization and increase warehouse capacity rather than to relocate immediately. A company can frequently extend the life of an existing facility for two or more years through an operational assessment to identify possible reconfigurations. Though even this level of internal change may be disruptive, it does not compare to moving to a new facility and training a new workforce.

Warehouse automation and software

Companies of all sizes are looking for warehouse automation that can provide an acceptable return on investment. This may entail redesigning distribution centers, operating processes, and systems to improve capacity and throughput and to lower the cost per order. A WMS is critical to enabling the design of new processes.

Return on investment

Many CFOs now require a 12–18 month payback on major capital projects. To achieve this, businesses need to perform a benefit analysis that includes hard savings and intangibles. Some companies are looking for ways to increase capacity for the future, rather than to reduce costs immediately.

Late holiday ordering

Many consumer businesses are heavily dependent on the Oct.–Dec. holiday period to produce the majority of their sales and profits. Customers have been buying closer to the actual holiday, causing larger sales spikes. This means that businesses must consider hiring and training of seasonal workers not only for higher peaks but for shorter periods. One way to deal with the issue is to stay in contact with good part-time workers throughout the year—pay them an incentive to come back. Pay them an incentive to stay through the season. Hire workers earlier so there is time to train them. Create management structure—temporary managers—to get through the peak. Some companies are successfully using temp agencies to take up this slack, but to make agencies work requires building a year-around relationship.

Multichannel operations

More companies are opening retail stores and selling wholesale in addition to catalog and e-commerce channels. Each channel has different requirements in terms of order processing, and corresponding warehouse processes should reflect these differences. Many fulfillment operations have had to become more complex in order to process small-order pick, pack, and ship or shift to larger regular store replenishment or large wholesale orders.

Outsourcing fulfillment

Finding a good match with a third-party fulfillment provider is becoming more difficult because of consolidations, changes in marketing direction by providers, and volatility in client–third-party relationships related to costs and service levels. One way is to use structured methodology for bidding out such work: evaluation and selection of vendors, including an RFP, site visits, and reference check. Be sure the vendor you choose has experience with your product type and order volume.

Customer service

Repeat business requires complete customer satisfaction. Direct customers expect merchants to ship their orders the same day that an order is placed, or at least the next day, they expect to receive the order in good condition, and they do not tolerate a negative performance (see service level metrics in the table Fulfillment Operations Metrics). As noted earlier, Q4 holiday customers are ordering later each year. This pattern of delayed purchase is a trend for which merchants must plan in order to secure repeat business. Everyone in the company needs to understand service level metrics, which should be reported just like productivity metrics. Fulfillment delivers on your company's marketing and merchandising promises. Promise realistically and over-deliver.

Warehouse inventory management

Increased attention to inventory management is another trend. Customer service improves as the initial order fill rate improves, and the cost of operations declines when a business no longer spends time looking for lost or unavailable inventory and no longer incurs the cost of expedited delivery to offset missed shipping dates. Accurate inventory removes barriers to productivity that other activities use as a crutch for poor performance. Four critical factors: Know what you own; how much, and where it is, and locate products in the most advantageous area.

Reducing the cost of inbound and outbound freight

When you look at major direct expenses, the cost of freight is possibly the most volatile. This year, following the postal rate increase, almost every company is directly addressing the cost of freight.

If you're a company assessing how to lower costs through competitive bidding you need to evaluate multiple carriers. Cost reduction is important, but so are service plans and customer service. Investigate inbound and outbound consolidation. Use a consultant experienced in negotiating with carriers to reduce costs. For outbound freight, use rate-shopping and best-way shipping. Inbound: Use collect rather than vendor-paid or prepaid.

Supply chain

Merchants seeking to optimize the supply chain is enlisting vendors to do as much as possible, with the idea that vendors can do it more cheaply, and that pre-processed products will move through the center more quickly. Vendors can provide value-added services such as marking, packaging for retail/direct, color/size sortation, etc. Merchants are also looking to push quality assurance up the supply chain, catching and correcting errors while a product is still in the vendor's factory. More and more companies are adopting electronic purchase orders, advanced shipping notices (ASNs), and drop-ship systems to connect the retailer and drop-ship vendors. More and more companies are strengthening their vendor compliance policies and manuals.

China import problems

At our September 2007 Forecasting and Inventory ShareGroup, inventory control managers expressed concerns about public safety, citing recalls over the last few months of Chinese-manufactured toys and household goods that contain lead. They were concerned about negative effects on consumer buying, increased testing of products at Chinese government-approved labs, and a slowdown in exports. We are sure that as companies (many now import over 50% of the products they sell) become more diligent about product specifications and testing, other problems in other countries may surface, and this will probably result in slower import lead times and some lost sales. Businesses need to improve product specifications and require proof of independent testing. They need to think through with the merchants what such changes could mean to receipts and customer service.

Summary

These are challenging times but also exciting times for companies as the direct industry changes, adapting to become truly multichannel and simultaneously responding to the expectations of customers and to the need to make a profit. If there's one element in this mix that does not change, it is the fact that productivity and customer service go hand in hand.

Rising Transportation Costs -
And What To Do About Them

By Bob Betke

For most multichannel merchants, transportation of goods is the highest operational expense. Inbound freight costs for domestically sourced product typically range from 2%-4% of gross sales, while for imported product, inbound freight costs 6% to 12% of gross sales. Outbound transportation costs typically average 6% to 8% of net sales.

And these costs are going up. FedEx recently announced a 6.9% increase in its net average shipping rate for FedEx Express, offset by a 2% reduction in fuel surcharge and a net increase of 4.9% on paper.

Parcel carriers always rate rates at the end of the year, more increases will be announced in the next few weeks. But labor issues could be pushing costs higher this year.

For instance, the courts have recently ruled FedEx drivers can file class action suits to reclassify them as company employees rather than independent contractors and thus eligible for benefits not currently paid them. United Parcel Service just reached an early labor agreement with the Teamsters Union equating to increased costs of $9.00 per hour in wages and benefits over five years. The value exceeds the 2002 UPS and Teamsters contract of $9.0 billion for six years.

The new UPS agreement calls for average annual wage and benefits increases of $1.80 per hour; the 2002 agreement averaged $1.46 per hour wage and benefit increases. Starting pay for UPS workers increases to $16.10 and workers with 24 months seniority increase to $20.75. Right now, the highest-paid UPS driver earns about $28.00 per hour.

What's more, under the new contract UPS agreed to pay the Teamsters $6 billion to allow UPS to withdrawal from the Teamsters Central States Pension fund. UPS will pay the costs of establishing a new pension fund for the involved participants.

Bottom line: The multichannel industry depends on parcel carriers and these providers' prices continually increase at rates higher than most other costs. What's your plan to deal with and reduce these expenses?

Here are a few tips from the MCM Live Webinar "Reducing Transportation Costs" I presented last week. You can click on the above link to review the full webinar.

Look at transportation in the context of the total supply chain efficiency. A few examples: implement vendor compliance to aid in product flow-through the distribution center, push compliance up the supply chain, implement vendor added-value services to reduce costs and speed product through the DC, build transportation into facility design, and implement supply chain IT systems to provide more timely and accurate information.

Institute vendor compliance policies, include routing guides for inbound carriers. Do not permit vendor-controlled freight, which can cost you 20% more.

For high returns businesses, such as apparel, use return services to process them more efficiently and provide a customer service.

Join an inbound freight consortium with contracted carriers and negotiated best rates. Get audited invoices and consolidated billing to your business while saving money.

Do your homework. You have to understand your volume and shipping characteristics, contract pricing, the 70-plus accessorial charges, available technology, rebate incentives, ground minimums, service level guarantees; available value-added services—to name just a few things that affect rates.

Consider a freight consultant, which can reduce costs 15% to 25%. Keep in mind the carriers have teams of pricing professionals negotiating your contract. Do you have the internal expertise to deal with these complexities and changes that determine your shipping costs? Specialized freight consulting firms will do a study, recommend areas for negotiation and contract structure, and make a commitment to savings up front.

The Price Of Free Holiday Shipping

By Curt Barry

Q: I am the operations manager of a large multichannel hardgoods and apparel merchant. My rough shipping and processing calculations for our company in Q4 this year would have been: 1) $70 million - $72 million gross revenue collected from shipping and processing, 2) $52 million - $54 million outbound shipping expenses, and 3) $18 million - $20 million net profit attributed to shipping and processing.

I say "would have been" because I just found out that we have started offering our customers unconditional free shipping and processing to entice holiday shoppers to start buying now. So my company is willing to pay out roughly $54 million in shipping fees as well as lose the estimated $20 million in net profit.

What are the underlying reasons behind offering free shipping and processing to customers? Is this common practice in other companies in the multichannel industry? Can anything positive come from giving free shipping to our customers?

A: You're correct that shipping and processing costs tend to be a rather large percent of sales. It is typically 6% to 8% of the average order, while shipping revenue is usually between 8% and 10% of the average order. So yes, the VP of Marketing is making your company cover the shipping and processing costs this holiday season as well as giving away revenue in order to get sales.

That's not necessarily a bad idea, however. We hear the complaint about free shipping from fulfillment and operations managers and directors all the time. Merchants must balance the use of free shipping and processing against the reality of the overall retail environment.

If your company is healthy, and you have a high average order value, you can afford to offer free shipping and processing. Other factors have to be in place for this enticement to work; such as having inventory available, adequate profit margins, productive and efficient operations, and deep outbound carrier discounts. What you really need to do is consider what the alternative might be.

We received an e-mail not long ago from a large, high-end multichannel women's apparel company offering 60% off all items. That's right: 60% off everything—in October. This is a clear indication of the kind of pressure multichannel businesses are under heading into the last two months of the year.

What's more, the order curve has been moving closer and closer to Christmas ever year, shifting a couple of days every year for the past 10 years. Peak weeks used to be in October, then shifted into November, and currently are in early December. This shift affects everybody, from forecasting to staffing. The fulfillment and distribution workforce that used to be packed up and home long before Christmas are now all working up to Dec. 23 to get the product out.

The reason for this shift? Customers are waiting until later in the season to get the best deals, as they know that retailers are going to start dropping their prices as it gets closer to the holiday. Those retailers who offer free shipping early on are trying to jumpstart orders and get the customers shopping earlier.

The idea is to attempt to move that curve back. If you get the customer shopping earlier, you're essentially taking dollars out of the holiday pot that they'd be spending elsewhere, because there's only so much money that's going to be spent in the holiday season.

Fulfillment and operations managers have just as much interest in moving that curve back as well. You want to get the shipping started early as well, so you don't have the influx of orders and having to cram six weeks of shipping into two weeks.

Though free shipping and processing seems a big chunk of money you're losing, it may be necessary to get those sales, get the shipping started, and spread that shipping out over the fourth quarter of the year.

Look at the example we used of the large women's apparel company, and ask yourself: Isn't free shipping and processing better than losing 60% of the revenue of the item itself? It really is a balancing act for each company that goes down the road of free shipping and processing.

Improving Outbound Freight Contracts

By Bob Betke

Q: My outbound freight to ship packages now exceeds my direct labor costs. I can't seem to control the expense. What can I do to reduce it?

A: Outbound freight exceeding the direct labor for fulfillment is a fact in many businesses. Here are some ways to reduce those expenses. Outbound freight costs continue to rise, but it is possible for direct marketers to optimize their situations. The good news is that all carrier contracts can be improved—most contracts have a short-term termination clause.

However, there are two important steps you must take to achieve all or part of the potential improvement: 1) You have to know more about your distribution than the carrier does, and 2) you must honestly assess whether your company has the knowledge and skills to negotiate a better contract, or whether you will do better with the help of a qualified consultant. First, you must understand a few things about your distribution:

- Know your annual spend and historical volume.
- Understand your carrier's contract pricing and incentives.
- Leverage your volume—single-sourcing yields a discount.
- Understand accessorial charges—these could be up to 40% of spend and more than 40 different charges.

- Use technology. Get on electronic invoicing so you can see the information necessary to negotiate effectively and have access to the same information the carrier has.

How do you make sure you have access to this critical information? To begin with, it is important to partner with the right carrier for your business. One important factor in choosing a carrier is to identify the right individual to be your account representative: a good representative will help achieve better service and optimum performance for you. Your rep should ensure that you receive effective management reports and schedule quarterly business reviews.

These quarterly reviews should be detailed accounts of your volume and charges, not simply social visits. These reviews can help you better understand the cost of performance. Your contract entitles you to professional service. Your carrier and account representative should be willing to work with you to perform the value-added services they provide, for example, a packaging analysis to optimize your performance and to reduce costs.

Some of the many contract details to review are:

- discount rates.
- rebate incentives
- ground minimums
- revenue qualifiers
- quick payment discount
- service-level guarantees and subsequent performance
- value-added services available to you
- benefits of automation (electronic invoicing)
- accessorial charges

Assuring that you have a quick payment discount is one easy and automatic method of cost reduction. Routine auditing of your invoices is critical to ensuring that you are invoiced correctly and that the carrier is performing to contractual service levels. It is conceivable that an audit of your invoices might identify invoice errors of 4% or higher in the carrier's favor. Skilled and knowledgeable auditing of your invoices guarantees that you receive all the benefits of your agreement with the carrier. The question is whether you have the skill and knowledge within your company to perform these invoice audits effectively.

That brings up the second key to improving your carrier agreement. Your outbound freight costs are one of your greatest operating costs. There is no room for pride or a false sense of knowledge when you are negotiating the terms for cost of operation. Be honest with yourself. If you or your company does not possess the skills and knowledge to effectively negotiate all the terms of the agreement discussed above and more, or if you do not possess the skills and knowledge to perform a monthly audit of your invoices—get help.

Warehouse Cost Reduction: Immediate Results

By Bob Betke

A common thread to all warehouse operations is the quest to manage expenses. The most critical and the most manageable expense item on your P&L statement is labor, and managing labor efficiently will generate immediate results in your work to manage expenses.

Managing labor begins with capturing daily man hours utilized by department or by activity in categories such as receiving, putaway, replenishment, pick/pack/ship, inventory management, supervision, etc. Capturing the man hours utilized can be done using sophisticated warehouse management system software or by a more manual approach, but no matter the method you use, you must know how many man hours are utilized each day in each activity.

Once you have successfully determined man hours utilized by activity, begin relating the man hours to a volume measurement (units, lines, orders, cases, pallets) for the activity by day. If you do not have a sophisticated system to do the calculation, create a spreadsheet for each activity with weeks down the side and days of the week across the top headings. Include subheadings for each day: volume, man hours, and volume per man hour. Total the horizontal subheadings for the week and calculate the total average week's performance. Charting this data cumulatively by day and week not only creates a management tool to begin monitoring and controlling labor expense, but it also develops a historical planning tool for budgeting.

Now that you have captured the core data of man hours utilized and volume by activity, the next step is to establish metrics of performance for each activity. Again the level of sophistication for developing performance metrics varies from industrially engineered labor standards to simply establishing reasonable expectations by making three to six observations of employees performing a task, averaging units per time, and deriving an expected performance level of units per man hour. Acceptable performance levels might include work pace averaging, performance rating, fatigue and delay allowance, control start and stop time, assessing the skill level of the employee performing the task, a detailed description of the activity, and identifying order(s) and units. It is beneficial to draw upon benchmarking information as reference to your own performance measurement.

The next step is to begin monitoring actual individual performance by day by activity or at least by core activity (the point at which the employee spends the most time performing work). Utilize the same type of spreadsheet and begin posting actual performance man hours and units to standard or reasonable expectations. One to three weeks' accumulation of data will clearly identify who is and who is not performing to expectation, and will also confirm if your standard is valid or if it requires review and adjustment. Your first obligation to underperforming employees is to assure that they are properly trained to perform the work effectively. Once assured they are trained you can effect management control within your company policies and guidelines either to improve their performance or replace them.

With performance measurement and planning tools in place you are ready to address the most immediate return to labor management— eliminate or reduce overtime or premium labor hours. Premium labor hours are a crutch for poor performance. We have found that the best method of reducing overtime operationally is to simply bite the bullet and advise your team that there will be no overtime unless you personally approve it, and you don't plan to do so. Typically, within a week or two following this direction you will find that the same work is being done with fewer man hours, and you will realize immediate savings. The downside to prepare for is that during those two weeks customer service will slip until all realize that you are serious and pick up the pace. The key to success in managing overtime is not to waver during those two weeks by approving exceptions to your rule.

Cross-Border Commerce

By Bob Betke

Q: I need a local fulfillment operation in Canada to effectively grow my business there. How would I proceed to develop an external fulfillment operation in Canada?

A: First and foremost, you have to develop a business model for the designated selling area. This is a three- to five-year strategic plan comprised of historical data and a projected forecast. A few pieces to the model are:

- Three to five years projected sales as orders, detailed to a weekly/daily (where appropriate) plan

- Average units and lines per order shipped

- Seasonal or peak volume increases as orders shipped, average lines per order, average units per line, average cartons per order

- Method of shipment and percentage of volume by type for purchase orders (small parcel, LTL, T/L, container)

- Preferred method(s) of shipping by percent of total volume

- Average weight per order shipped

Second, identify where your projected concentration of sales will be and determine the most advantageous physical location within the new selling area for a fulfillment operation for your projected business model. Site selection is critical to managing shipping costs and to assuring there is an adequate labor pool.

Third, decide whether you should handle your own fulfillment or contract a third-party logistics provider. You must identify any tax implications related to opening a new business as an employer. Normally the least-cost method of establishing a new operation is with a 3PL provider. Unless tax concessions for new employers are significant and long-term, it will likely be more economical to operate for the first two to three years with a third party. You can use the Internet to identify potential 3PLs. However, we definitely recommend a visit to prospective partners as a preliminary to any further conversation. It is much better to have a visual image later as you review respective proposals.

Third-party fulfillment

If you do decide to explore contracting with a 3PL, you must develop a request for proposal. The primary content of the RFP is your business model. The more accurate the information you supply about your business, the more effective the proposals from 3PLs will be. Send the RFP, with a clear deadline, to three to six 3PLs that you believe are stable, industry-proven, and can effectively handle the volume from your business.

It is important to identify clearly every statement of what the candidates propose to do and not to do, and every requirement and cost within a proposal. Establish a spreadsheet so you can compare proposals and details. If your team does not possess the experience to review and negotiate agreements, pursue the services of a consultant. Next you have to negotiate all the standards of work and contract terms to assure that the 3PL can actually provide the service you expect.

Your work is not complete even after you have negotiated an agreement. Developing a successful 3PL partnership requires a significant amount of time, effort, and follow-up by the client company. You need to make clear that you have relinquished only the physical handling of your product to the 3PL, not the responsibility to manage your business.

Identify key client contacts and decision-makers who will be issuing direction to the 3PL. The 3PL provider needs to clearly understand who will provide direction and who is responsible for resolving problems.

Remember that the 3PL is proud of how it manages its business. Use the same consideration communicating with the 3PL that you would extend to your most valued associates inside your own company. Never ignore issues or problems, but be firm and respectful in resolving them. The 3PL is normally quite aware of who is paying the bills and who owns the inventory. The 3PL exists to serve; you should be a gracious ruler.

Communicate daily with 3PL management and visit the site as frequently as travel restrictions permit. Discuss the basics of the previous day's operations—receiving, shipping, inventory management—and always inquire what you can do to assist them to achieve their goals and objectives. If possible, visit monthly, but no less than quarterly. This sort of relationship can become a classic case of "out of sight, out of mind."

The client has to be diligent in managing the 3PL through daily reporting. You are now managing a remote location, and therefore your best source of information is the 3PL's daily reporting and invoices. This is no different than managing your own operation. Master the information reporting so you can identify trends and immediately spot issues as they appear.

Inventory management is the most important reporting in managing a 3PL. The client has to know where to look for issues such as lost or damaged inventory, out-of-stock, and when the inventory records indicate adequate supply. These are indications of performance concerns requiring the client's follow-up and resolution.

Receiving performance reports and inbound scheduling are next in importance for daily follow-up. The client has to know if there are vendor delivery problems or 3PL receiving issues that will affect the customer service level. This is also where the daily phone follow-up will indicate any "carry-over" receiving issues on a purchase order.

Normal daily shipping follow-up is important, but the most important point is to know what did not ship.

Returns reporting is crucial not only to identifying customers' satisfaction with your product, but also to discovering any 3PL –related performance issues. Detailed reason code reporting is imperative, and cumulative graphing is valuable in discussions with the 3PL.

Growing a business by expanding operations to Canada is an exciting and challenging prospect. If you take the time to lay the groundwork by developing a comprehensive business model and researching site selection and possible 3PL involvement carefully, you will significantly reduce the challenges and increase your chances of success.

Expanding Existing Warehouse Capacity

By Bob Betke

Many of the warehouse assessments that F. Curtis Barry & Company performs are initiated because a client perceives that its warehouse is out of space for receiving and storing product or creating more pick locations, thus limiting the growth of the business. Our approach to interacting with the client is to provide an experienced, fresh set of eyes to view the current layout and to envision potential revisions with the intent of gaining two to five more years in the existing facility.

Here are the top 14 elements we review when assessing a current warehouse layout.

1. Thoroughly understand the flow and utilization of the current layout, including rack configuration, slotting/pick philosophy, receiving, putaway, replenishment, inventory management, and packing and shipping. Include peak seasonal trends and a thorough volume analysis of inbound and outbound product flow.

2. Identify the dimensions of the footprint as well as the clear height. Are there physical impediments to change? What are the characteristics of the building? How does the building dictate or impair the process flow from receiving through shipping?

3. How do you utilize the available space? Look for storage racks

that do not utilize the clear height; pick areas used as flow rack without overhead storage above them; conveyor located on the floor that inhibits the use of high cube area or the flow of product; or offices or work areas located in potential high cube areas.

4. How does the current design and practice of product storage configuration and pick location configuration lend itself to efficient utilization? Example: It's great to use flow rack for high-volume picking, but underutilized depth of flow rack potential space is wasted and lost.

5. In addition to pick, pack, and ship, does the warehouse incorporate processes such as kitting, value-added processes, imprinting on demand, or manufacturing? Do you store raw material and finished goods?

6. Does product move efficiently from the receiving area, or are there delays—either vendor-created or client-created?

7. Does the current material handling equipment operate effectively in the current environment? Will it function efficiently in the revised layout?

8. What are the capabilities and restrictions of the system used today? What will be required to advance the system's capability to support new flow processes? For instance, systems must be capable of supporting barcode scanning.

9. How many dock doors are there? Do you use the same door/s for both shipping and receiving? What is the schedule of activity for both functions?

10. Consider the work schedule. How many employees can function

effectively during a shift? How many shifts are required to complete the various activities? The goal is to achieve maximum utilization of the material handling equipment and fixed assets.

11. Does the operation require off-site storage and related processes?

12. Do you apply performance metrics and manage a performance reporting program to assure maximum utilization of your most valuable asset—the employees?

13. Analyze how effectively the inventory management program maintains accuracy to eliminate wasted and lost time in order fulfillment and returns processing. Does the product line present shelf life concerns?

14. Once you have decided to initiate changes, identify what changes should be initiated immediately and completed within three to six months and which changes require longer to implement and complete. It's equally important to determine which action items are capital-intensive. These may be either necessary or secondary but will be required in the long term.

How To Diagnose Inventory Accuracy Issues

By Bob Betke

Q: If you were asked to choose the one operational area in the distribution center that could generate the greatest improvement in performance, which would it be?

A: Two words: inventory accuracy. I believe managing inventory accuracy is the greatest single contributor to improving performance and customer service and reducing cost.

Consider all the potential rework you could eliminate if your inventory were accurate: Product would be available to fulfill orders on demand; orders would be completed in one pass and not rehandled; you wouldn't have to waste labor tracing product movement history and searching for lost product within the DC; packing and shipping personnel could work at a more consistent pace without delay.

Most inventory management problems are reactive rather than proactive. Proactive inventory management that results in accuracy levels greater than 99.75 % have two key process requirements and a host of support processes.

Key requirement number one: Assure the product is correctly identified and correctly received on the inbound dock. This requires both vendor and DC participation. In the DC, associates holding the critical position of receiver are the first level of proactive inventory management. They need to be part dictator and part accountant. Receivers must be enabled to correctly identify to the minutest detail all pertinent SKU, quantity, and description information. I believe this job should carry a premium hourly rate, perhaps the highest in the DC. To retain the position, a receiver should not make more than two errors in a rolling six-month period; if he does, he should be removed from the job.

Key requirement number two: Perform aisle mapping or location auditing daily. Everyone says, "We do that, and we still have problems," but if you just follow this prescription, your problems will begin to disappear. Develop a report enabling the printing of one side of an aisle in location sequence (or in RF technology the downloading) to a handheld. Identify for each location the SKU number and the description, pack, size, and color that is called for in the inventory. The quantity in the location is optional. The basis of the solution is to verify that the correct item is in the location called for.

Work through half of an aisle at a time so that the process is manageable and you can make timely corrections to discrepancies. Identify conscientious, detail-oriented associates (the number will depend on the size of the DC) and have them begin mapping the first aisle of reserve product and follow it through the last aisle, completing the cycle in two weeks. Then begin all over again. You should perform the same sort of mapping in pick locations.

Support processes: It is important to place responsibility for inventory management with the strongest manager on your team to ensure consistency of application and accuracy of detail. Applying cycle-counting programs is beneficial when that application is based on A/B/C volume analysis and counts every identified location of an SKU. RF technology using barcodes at every possible application is an excellent counting method, including but not limited to SKU identification, verification of the put-away location, tracking product location throughout the facility, pick verification, and pack verification. Directed put-away as part of a warehouse management system helps to clear up many blemishes. I recommend a daily condition report indicating all inventory adjustments by SKU, plus or minus, units, dollars, reason, and who made the adjustment. I also like to see total weekly adjustments as a percentage of total inventory expressed as both units and dollars and graphed to identify trends.

Q: But why is inventory management the most important source for generating operational improvement?

A: Because implementing inventory management removes the most prevalent crutch for poor performance by holding all other DC employees to specific standards.

Fulfillment: The Key To Customer Satisfaction

By Curt Barry

Can you honestly say that your company is committed to customer satisfaction? Really and truly committed? You know that customer satisfaction is what keeps the orders flowing in, especially in direct-to-customer operations, hassle-free shopping is key to repeat business.

But are you doing everything you can to ensure customer satisfaction? Here in the States, it's become fashionable for companies to insist that service representatives address customers by name for a "personal touch". It's a good idea, but experience shows that what really matters to customers is that their orders get shipped out accurately and on time. And for that, you need to go beyond the cheery greeting. You need to go deep into your warehouse, and make sure that everything that goes on there supports customer satisfaction.

The warehouse is the oft-forgotten element in customer service. It's here that orders received by the customer contact center are executed: merchandise is accurately picked for individual shipments, packed to ensure against breakage and shipped according to the customer's instructions. It's here that shipments of goods are received and put away – in a manner, you hope, that makes them easy to retrieve. A mistake at any stage of the process can cost you customer trust and money, the latter in terms of correcting an error, and in the loss of future orders.

The rise of e-commerce has made a smoothly functioning warehouse more important than ever, as customer expectations for speedy delivery of goods have skyrocketed. If placing an order is as fast as point-and-click, fulfilling it should be just as fast, or so they assume. All the more reason for your warehouse to be operating at top efficiency.

How do you achieve that efficiency? How do you translate your commitment to customer satisfaction from intention to deed? How do you maintain your standards day in and day out? The key is to understand your warehouse operations on all levels:

- Why, as a direct-to-customer/small-order distribution center, it differs from other (retail-based) warehouses.

- How layout and design, and "engineering" of each task – from mapping of the simplest foot-traffic patterns to selection of sophisticated equipment and computer support, can streamline or stymie your fulfillment process.

- How you ensure you continue to meet customer expectations through regular operational audits and benchmarking, measuring your warehouse performance against industry and individualized internal standards.

The Direct-To-Customer/Small-Order Distribution Center

More retailers are moving into direct-to-consumer sales, either via catalog or the Internet. But catalogs and e-commerce enterprises have characteristics that differentiate them from retail operations. For the former, order sizes are smaller, requiring warehouse personnel to pick individual units.

Retail operations typically have longer lead-times to move goods and the advantage of being pre-scheduled, while catalog and e-commerce warehouses must cope with wildly changing demand, with little or no ability to accurately forecast order volume. Catalog and e-commerce warehouses are more static environments (goods remain in storage for longer periods), while retail warehouses tend to operate in flow-through style (with goods moving in and out constantly). To complicate the flow in the catalog and e-commerce warehouse, today's customers increasingly expect same-day order turnaround of individual orders.

Catalog and e-commerce warehouses have several other functions that retail warehouses don't: e.g., returns processing and cross-docking of back orders for individual SKUs. In addition, direct-to-customer warehouses have to facilitate a variety of shipping methods, depending on customer choice; this necessitates having the proper shipping manifesting systems in-house. Increasingly too, special value-added services designed to entice customers are executed in the warehouse.

Warehouse Design & Operations

The design of your warehouse and the operations standards and procedures you establish will have a tremendous effect on customer satisfaction. The best strategies, however, are often simple, basic common sense – so basic that they are often forgotten.

Many of these simple principles address efficiency. If you are wondering how that relates to customer service, keep in mind that increased productivity, speed and accuracy are the keys to customer satisfaction.

Maintain flexibility:

The first rule of improving the day-to-day operations is to stay flexible. Don 't be "married" to a particular layout or procedure. Cultivate an attitude of openness to new ideas and "better mousetraps". As your business grows, you'll be obliged to change aspects of your operation. In the meantime, flexibility will make constant improvement part of your working culture, and you and your staff will be ready for the day when circumstances force you to make changes.

Use the cube:

Your warehouse isn't just floor space or space that can be reached by the pick personnel standing on the floor. When designing storage, think "upwards"; use all the space. This may necessitate more elaborate racking and some form of sophisticated material-handling equipment, but such investments could well make your warehouse operate more cost-effectively in the long term.

Fit equipment and procedures to your product:

Let your product mix dictate methods for storage, slotting, picking and conveyance, not the other way around. Don 't decide you like one kind of slotting and struggle to make it work for all your merchandise. If your catalog or e-commerce site sells a variety of merchandise (soft goods that come in various sizes and colors, books and giftware, for instance) figure out what works best for each category. Then calculate how much of each you need based on the average merchandise mix and your customers' ordering patterns. Many direct-to-customer business software packages can perform this sort of analysis and generate reports to guide you.

Think traffic:

Plot out how and when merchandise moves through your warehouse. Walk through Picking and Packing – and don't forget Replenishment. Use the rule of thumb that you'll need one week's average sales of all "A" items in primary pick locations and allow for enough space in and easy access to those locations. Consider your replenishment patterns: do you favor demand replenishment (replenishment based on order trends) min-max controls (automatic replen-ishment when quantities reach predetermined levels) or both? Factor this into your traffic plan – and then factor your traffic plan into design and operations strategies.

Be tidy and avoid congestion:

Avoiding congestion isn't just a matter of cosmetics; cluttered aisles really can slow down the movement of goods through the warehouse. Also, a disorganized, cluttered warehouse leads to more frequent – and costly – errors. Avoiding this means keeping up with receiving, putaway and replenishment, and not letting merchandise accumulate in the aisles; your warehouse staff will move more efficiently and be less prone to costly accidents. It also means allowing for enough accumulation space where needed. At the receiving dock, for example, if you don't have enough space to put the goods that are being off-loaded and staged for putaway, once that space is filled, work will cease. The same is true of space to accumulate completed orders that are packed for shipping. A good rule of thumb is to assume you will keep 10 percent of primary picking and reserve storage locations empty; that way, during peak times, if they do fill up, they won't over-flow.

Minimize travel time:

Most of your warehouse staff's time is spent traveling back and forth, so make every step count. Batch and route work assignments to minimize unproductive travel time; sort orders in a variety of ways, depending on customer and business needs (regular vs. overnight shipment or singles vs. multi-line orders). In many cases, direct-to-customer business software packages or warehouse management software packages can do the sorting and routing according to your specifications. Equip your staff with the right material-handling tools so they can carry as much as possible on a given trip. Consider conveyor belts if they are feasible and cost-effective for your operation. (There's a wide range of kinds and prices, from gravity powered conveyors to fully automated.) Save an entire step in the process by cross-docking whenever possible; that is, if a back-ordered item arrives, send it directly to the packing area so it can be shipped immediately, rather than moving it through putaway, replenishment and picking first.

Stress Accuracy:

Speed means nothing if the wrong items are shipped out. Lack of accuracy costs you in both customer satisfaction and money to correct your mistake. Use bar codes and scanners as much as possible in receiving, picking, packing and shipping. Make quality control a non-negotiable part of the packing process; have packers double-check orders or use your computer system's pack-verification function before they are packed to correct any mistakes.

Schedule wisely:

Approach scheduling like an engineer. When does it make the most sense to do which task? Staggering work schedules increases productivity. Have the pickers start their day a little before the packers, because when the packers start, they have orders to work with the minute they hit their workstations. Likewise, replenishment is more efficient when performed off-shift – that is, when the replenishers won't bump into the picking crew. It's a balancing act, but worth it.

Auditing and benchmarking:

Once you arrive at a warehouse design and operational procedures, don't stop there. Customer satisfaction requires that you be vigilant about maintaining the standards that you have set, and – especially in the instant-gratification culture of e-commerce – improving on them. Two analytical tools can help you in this endeavor: regular operations audits (productivity, cost and quality measurements of every task in the warehouse) and benchmarking (numeric comparisons of your performance against internal standards and that of comparable companies).

Audit your performance:

Measure productivity throughout the ware-house. Calculate units of merchandise processed per hour by various departments, accuracy of shipments (based on returns), order turnaround time, cost of labor and other costs. Include everything: labor, physical plant and equipment, computer systems and procedures. Analyze these figures to create key operating reports for measuring performance. Note any trends over time. Analyze the audit observations and create action plans for improvement.

Make a physical audit of the warehouse:

Create a template to define areas and issues to check your physical audit. This is the road map you will follow when you make regular tours of the facility.

Note conditions such as the organization of the plant, condition of the equipment, organization and completion of paperwork, work pace, working conditions such as lighting, heat, ventilation and cleanliness and morale.

Compare yourself with external benchmarks:

Review industry-wide benchmarks for comparable companies (available in industry publications, at seminars, from fellow catalog professionals and consultants). Compare these with your own performance statistics. Do you measure up?

Set the standards you would like to achieve:

Using industry benchmarks and your own unique operating characteristics as a guide, set your own standards. Put them in writing so you can refer to them in the future, and make sure your employees are aware of them. Conduct a systematic search for areas of potential improvement.

Make auditing and benchmarking part of your routine:

Don't just measure performance and set goals for improvement once. Schedule regular reviews, major and minor, throughout the year.

Compare your goals to actual performance. Your warehouse plays a major role in the satisfaction of your customers.

By paying attention to the basics of efficient design and operations and measuring performance regularly, you can boost customer satisfaction, and ultimately, profits.

Opportunities For Improvement Of Your Inbound Freight Management Process

By Bob Betke

Some things never change. After the Holiday season, there is invariably a movement to determine how costs can be reduced for the upcoming year. Every aspect of the operation should and does come under review. But, not every area of the business is given equal scrutiny. The following information discusses one of those areas that traditionally do not receive the attention they deserve.

Management of the inbound freight function is one of the most overlooked areas for significant cost reduction in many companies. Direct marketing companies may spend from 2 – 4% of gross sales on inbound freight. Some estimates rate inbound freight costs as 35% of the total logistics cost of many companies. Remember that any savings in inbound freight costs can go directly to the bottom line. Most successful companies who have paid attention to inbound freight view inbound freight management as controlling inventory in transit. Since your inventory is, in many cases, your largest asset, the management of this asset is critical to your business success. The proper management of this function plays a key role in achieving inventory, productivity, and service goals.

Inbound freight involves the management and control of freight from domestic and offshore vendors, consolidation of vendor shipments, direct shipments to Retail sites and customers at home, multiple shipping points, and warehouse cross dock opportunities for Retail replenishment and backorder processing. The variety of processes supported by the inbound freight process make its management a complex undertaking.

Effectively managing the inbound flow of product to your business is a complicated process. It is becoming more complex as customer demands increase in terms of their expectations of service levels. Compounding the difficulty is management's desire to effect cost reduction while maintaining reliable service. In addition to the more obvious and visible impact of inbound freight costs to overall profitability, the management of this area also affects inventory control, overall warehouse productivity, and customer service.

Making matters even more difficult are issues such as rising fuel charges, the increase in offshore product sourcing, and the ever changing array of carriers and their service offerings. Adding to the difficulty is the increasing phenomenon of multi channel businesses operating out of multiple warehouse facilities. In addition, direct shipments to Retail locations and Direct customers make controlling inbound activities in a cost effective manner much more complex.

As you begin to analyze your inbound freight practices, you should establish objectives that will help guide your decision making process. Objectives can be established in the following areas; among others:

1. Reduced freight costs and improved "bottom line"
2. Improvement in on-time deliveries
3. Reduction in purchasing lead times
4. Less handlings and damage
5. Lower inventory levels and reduced carrying costs
6. Providing maximum visibility into the process
7. Improvement in warehouse productivity

8. Increased customer service

In order to meet your objectives, there are a few key areas of attention that can provide the focus for the analysis. Four key issues or areas that warrant your attention are:

1. Vendor Compliance
2. Freight Paid vs. Freight Collect
3. Visibility and System Control
4. Vendor Relationships

1. Vendor Compliance

Having a current and complete Vendor Compliance program lies at the heart of inbound freight management. The program should, most importantly, define vendor expectations and provide for a method of measuring and reporting on performance against those expectations. It is one of the most effective ways to insure consistency and reliability in the management of the inbound freight process.

Basic measures such as on-time delivery, meeting damage and accuracy expectations, and providing the proper paperwork are among the key metrics to monitor. With the increase in imported product and the diversity of domestic vendors and an increasing use of consolidators, providing a routing guide is a critical piece of any Vendor Compliance program. By controlling the routing and timing of deliveries from your vendors, efficiencies throughout the supply chain are possible.

2. Freight Paid vs. Freight Collect

There is a growing trend in the industry to convert from the prepaid freight concept to a freight collect policy. Those who have performed the due diligence of the comparison of these two concepts are realizing significant cost reductions and overall control. They have realized the words "Free Freight" should raise a red flag and precipitate further discussion.

Although it is sometimes very difficult to gather the required information to make an informed decision, the effort can be well worth your time. Even if there are no changes made, the discussions you have with your vendors and carriers often prove beneficial in other areas.

3. Visibility and System Control

One of the key elements in an effective inbound freight management process is the ability to have visibility into the supply chain to track and control inventory movements. This control has to be supported by an information system that helps manage this complex process.

Many software vendors offer products that help manage the process in a variety of ways. You should always develop a set of functional and process requirements that you expect the software to meet before you begin the search. During the search, an evaluation of their responses to these requirements and a combination of reference calls, site visits, and system demos should be completed. Making sure you know what you want is the first step in obtaining a system that meets your needs and expectations.

4. Vendor Relationships

One of the most overlooked factors in a successful inbound freight program is the relationship you have with your vendors and carriers. Those companies who have taken the time to foster a productive and collaborative relationship consistently reap the benefits. As in any relationship, having a feeling of trust and the ability to have an honest and meaningful dialog are the keys to success.

Many companies try to manage the relationship through rigid contracts and performance measures. While these are important, having the ability to deal with someone you trust supersedes any legal restrictions you can place on the process. Many ideas for improving the process come through this dialog and collaboration, rather than through the strict enforcement of an agreement. In addition, with the speed at which the total supply chain is evolving, having a good relationship is a real asset in keeping up.

Those companies who have paid attention to the management of the inbound freight process have seen reductions in overall freight costs, reduced inventories and safety stock, improved warehouse operating costs, and enhanced overall customer service. It is worth the time and energy to investigate this often overlooked area in your supply chain.

Returns: It's An Operations And A Customer Issue

By Bob Betke

Analyze this: In deciding whether to shop direct or retail, 81% of consumers state that "ease of returns" as an important to their decision, according to a survey by Harris Interactive for Newgistics. The numbers are even more telling after a return is made- Harris Interactive found that 95% of customers are likely to shop with an online merchant again if the return process is convenient. What that says to marketers is that even if a customer returns a purchase, the experience can still be a positive one in terms of instilling loyalty.

It's important for direct marketers to recognize that operations issues such as merchandise returns are, in fact, marketing issues. Smart, customer-oriented marketers like L.L. Bean and Lands' End already know this and have always tried to make it as easy as possible on the customer if a return has to be made. Lifetime guarantees stating that a customer may return a product at any time, for any reason, go a long way toward making people feel secure about shopping by catalog or on the Web. Of course, at the end of any merchandise return, you, as the merchant, are still left with a piece of product sitting on your receiving dock, so the returns process must also be dealt with as an operational issue. In this article, we'll take a look at both the front end and back end of the returns process—and what you need to do to ensure a streamlined flow of the product from the customer back into the distribution center.

Depending on how much you want to invest in printing and processing labels, there are a variety of means available for getting returns from the customer back to you. Let's look at the options:

Pre-printed return labels, where the customer pays the postage, are the basic standard of the direct order industry. The merchant includes the proper instructions and pre-addressed labels to make the returns as easy as possible — even though the customer still must take the package to the post office or expedited carrier and pay for postage. This option costs you the least but puts the greatest burden on the customer. A variation of this method, where the merchant pays the postage, is the most costly option for the merchant and is usually used only by upscale retailers. Marketers such as Brooks Brothers elect to provide the service not only as a convenience to the customer but also as a benefit of shopping its catalog or Web site.

Smart Labels, offered by Newgistics Inc., enables deduction of the return postage fee from the customer's return merchandise credit; catalog customers simply detach the pre-addressed, bar-coded Smart-Label from their order summary, affix it to their package, and drop it off anywhere in the U.S. Postal Service (USPS) mail stream. Smart-Label's bar code links the package to the customer's invoice and provides package visibility to retailers early in the returns process.

Cross-channel returns options enable shoppers who have purchased from one channel to make a return through another. For example, Sears stores now accept Lands' End catalog returns, and Gap Inc. allows store returns of online purchases. Retailers with catalog operations presence and a reputation for excellent customer service, such as Neiman Marcus, Talbots and Cabela's, typically take back catalog returns at stores. (We will say that store managers may not be too pleased with that policy if the catalog and stores have different assortments.)

Smart Comebacks

Whether a returned item was the wrong size or was defective, you need a set of procedures for handling the product once it arrives back at your warehouse. This is called a reverse logistics strategy, and it accounts for what happens to all returned items from the time a customer decides she doesn't want a pair of jeans because they are missing a button to the time the pair of jeans is repaired and put back on the shelf for sale. Here are nine steps to implement an efficient reverse logistics strategy:

1. Create clear, understandable returns forms that are easy for both customers and your staff to use. Post the policies clearly in the FAQs on your Web site.

2. Design your workstations with efficiency in mind (including allowing room for removal of returned boxes and other trash). Consider the desired flow of product and provide sufficient operating space.

3. Provide adequate work and staging areas for returns.

4. Institute a simple three-part transaction: Process the credit refunds or exchanges; update the customer file; and determine the product disposition.

5. Train your staff on handling returns. Provide a training manual and sufficient time for employees to become comfortable with the process.

6. Make your company's written policies and procedures for returns accessible to all personnel at all times.

7. Use bar codes to identify product so that it can be returned to inventory or otherwise disposed of quickly and efficiently. Less keying means fewer errors.

8. Define return-to-stock procedures and be sure they are carried out in eight-hour to 24-hour cycles. Make sure enough space is allocated for storage of product to be returned to stock.

9. Cross-dock returns whenever possible. If the returned item is on backorder, you can ship it to the waiting customer rather than restocking it. Designate experienced personnel to make decisions on routing of returned merchandise; assign less experienced (and less costly) personnel to repetitive keying and packaging functions.

Processing returns carries high costs that affect several areas within your organization. Here's an example of the high price you might incur for processing one return of a $50 item: $8 to $13 for initial order processing and fulfillment, not including the shipping and handling costs, and another $8 to $10 for marketing, IT, merchandising and general/administrative costs. Plus, if your company's error prompted the return and you have to pay the shipping, add another $4 or more. Back-end costs tack on an additional $3 to $4. If you have to re-ship a new product and bear that cost as well, throw in another $4. And if the transaction is not an exchange, the entire profit margin of $27.50 (at 55% gross margin) is lost along with the processing costs cited above.

Good returns handling practices are important for another reason in addition to the straight cost factor. The high price tag of mishandling returns also carries the danger of a potential loss of customer loyalty. If your return costs are just too high to handle, you may want to consider outsourcing all or parts of the process.

Returns are an unavoidable part of direct marketing. They can cost a bundle in the short term, and if you manage them poorly, they'll cost even more in customer trust and loyalty over the long run. But by taking control of the process and streamlining it, you can minimize losses and satisfy your customers.

10 Ways To Improve Efficiency And Reduce Costs In Your Warehouse Operations

By Bob Betke

Absolute productivity has declined in many companies.

Indeed, in conducting our benchmarking surveys (which we've done since 1996), we've discovered that many metrics, such as orders processed per full-time warehouse worker, remained flat, while dollars of sales processed per warehouse square foot have declined. In turn, labor rates have increased from an average of $5.50 to $10.50 per direct labor hour. To help you boost productivity at your catalog, I'll focus on the warehouse audit process and the application of a few key warehouse success factors.

An Operations Audit

When trying to reduce costs and boost customer satisfaction and profits, first measure and analyze what's currently being done. To determine if your warehouse operation in particular is as efficient as it can be, start with a warehouse operations audit. Such an audit takes a quantitative and qualitative look at your fulfillment operation's productivity and accuracy, and does so in a systematic way.

A good operations audit enables you to measure warehouse productivity and other important metrics to identify patterns and trends. It also allows you to complete both internal and external comparisons. Once you gather the data and make comparisons, you'll be able to draft an action plan for improvement.

Unfortunately, there isn't a fail-safe, textbook approach to the operations audit. Many companies employ an independent resource to conduct the audit for an unbiased and independent perspective. (See sidebar: How To Select a Fulfillment Consultant).

The audit should consist of a method for evaluating your own operation against a set of internal expectations, as well as external, industry-accepted, best practices and averages (outlined below). Remember, you can't improve something if you don't measure it.

Using a template – that is, a list of predetermined key evaluation points – for each area of the warehouse can aid in the audit's organization. Focus on labor, facilities, systems and workflow procedures. By analyzing your operation against your existing expectations, you can develop a basis of measurement for future actions.

10 Critical Success Factors

The following is a list of key factors common to successful warehouse operations.

1. Use the cube.

Our studies show that occupancy (cost of space and utilities) ranges from 25 percent to 35 percent of the cost per order.

One of the single biggest culprits in optimization of your warehouse asset is not adequately using available cubic space. Your first look as you walk through the facility should be up.

Inefficient use of the available cube can translate into increased costs for additional warehouse space that you may not actually need. Typically, receiving, picking, packing and shipping generally use 40 percent to 50 percent of your space; product storage the remainder. Use racking, mezzanines, multilevel order-picking concepts and powered conveyor placement to increase your facility's utilization.

In addition, look at the cube use in your picking slots and reserve locations to determine if a space reconfiguration can boost the amount of products stored.

2. Ensure that sufficient product is available when a picker needs it.

Use a combination of scheduled replenishment of the primary pick slot utilizing the min-max and demand-replenishment concepts. Most warehouse management systems and some catalog order management systems support these concepts. However, a shortcoming of many catalog management systems is that the picking-ticket process assumes that the pick face has been restocked and product is available. This frequently can hinder picker's productivity.

3. Develop appropriate pick locations.

As much as 70 percent of a picker's work hours may be spent walking. Consider product velocity (sales movement) and size (cube) when selecting the picking slots sizes and location. Many operations replenish forward picking too often. Set up a system in which you can store at least one week's average unit movement in the pick slot and a "hot pick" area for extremely fast movers. Provide various slot sizes.

4. Take advantage of bar code technology -

from the receiving through the shipping functions. Among the many reasons to employ bar codes: You can track products and orders, verify accuracy, speed processes, gain early visibility, and eliminate paperwork. Develop an ROI study to show where savings can be gained.

5. Keep it clean and organized.

Generally, you can tell a lot about the type of warehouse operation in place just by looking at the facility's overall organization and appearance.

6. Plan for flexibility and scalability.

Any warehouse facility or system should be designed to maximize flexibility and be as scalable as possible. With increasing uncertainty about future business plans, it's mandatory that you remain flexible and able to respond to changing requirements, such as when merchants add SKUs or change the type of items and product profiles (sizes) they offer.

One of our clients recently gave us planned future operating metrics, which we used in our efforts to size a new warehouse for them. After studying the metrics, and the new facility's design, we realized they would be out of room in just six months. What happened? They had underestimated their future inventory levels by more than 100 percent.

In our planning, additional space was allocated for future expansions. This scalability permitted the warehouse to meet actual inventory needs without major difficulty. If the idea of scalability had not considered in the design, the lack of space would've been a critical issue.

7. Get an efficient stock-locator system.

This sounds like an elementary question, but do you know where all of your inventory is located? One shortcoming of some catalog management systems is that their warehouse inventory systems can show product inventory in only one location. Manual systems have to be used to record other locations for the same SKU. For efficient operations, your warehouse inventory system must be able to identify what product is stored in each location, as well as the quantity of each product in every location.

8. Devise a vendor-compliance program.

Everything starts at your warehouse's receiving door. Moreover, every function, from put-away to shipping, is impacted in some way by your vendors. That's why it's a good idea to devise and enforce a vendor-compliance program that defines the detailed expectations and specifications required of every vendor. The program also should include corrective processes to be used and ramifications for non-compliance.

Take vendor packaging. If a vendor fails to comply with acceptable and agreed upon packaging specifications, the following situations may occur:

- Products designated as shipalones (i.e., items reshipped in the original packaging) may have to be repacked, creating increased labor costs for you.
- Bar code labels on the vendor packaging may not be reusable (readable) in the warehouse, thereby decreasing accuracy and increasing handling costs.
- You could incur actual damage to your warehouse from products

arriving improperly packaged.

9. Measure and report performance metrics to your workers.

The old axiom, "You can't improve what you don't measure," still is true in warehouse operations. The simple act of measuring operating metrics and reporting the results to your employees will result in an improvement — even if you do nothing else with the data. Why? Most employees just want to know how they're doing. By setting expectations and then telling everyone how they're measuring up, you can improve overall productivity.

Takeaway tip: Set up productivity measurements in units and cost for all major departments (e.g., receiving, stocking, replenishment).

10. Maximize what you have before investing in a new solution.

If you attribute savings or improvements to a new investment when those same improvements could've been obtained with a review/ modification of your existing process, the payback or justification for the investment is inflated.

Some Operational Averages

Once you've completed your existing operational analysis, compare yourself to some industry averages. Here are a few key metrics from a cross section of some of the better-run companies in the direct-to-customer industry. Keep in mind these averages come from different-sized merchants selling apparel and/or hard-goods product lines.

Warehouse cost per order:

Good productivity is around $4 per order (which includes direct and indirect labor, occupancy costs and packaging). Highly efficient businesses may be as low as $2.25. However, we've seen highly automated facilities that don't yield low cost per order when the systems investment wasn't well planned or when product type varied widely.

Order processing turnaround times:

The time to pick, pack and ship an order is 24 hours or less. Since the dot-com revolution, however, many businesses are processing 50 percent or more of orders the same day.

Returns and receiving processing turnaround times:

Within 24 hours.

Functional area productivity:

Picking averages 115 units per man-hour, and packing is 36 boxes per man-hour for conventional warehouses. But small-product picking rates may range from 275 to 800 units per hour. Highly automated facilities may achieve picking of 150 to 175 units per hour, and packing of 75 to 90 boxes per hour. Of course, compare your business and those that are similar to yours.

Orders per square foot:

6.5 is the average.

Net sales per square foot of warehouse space:

$750 is the average, and varies by product size and value. This is down from $1,000 net sales per square foot 10 years ago, even though most companies' average order sizes have increased.

Orders per full-time equivalent employee:

15 to 17.

Conclusion

An operational audit is an ongoing initiative that can help continuously improve your company's productivity. Process the audit's results and the corresponding ideas and opportunities for change. Compare your business to those that are similar in size and type. Then prioritize and schedule your anticipated changes in a manageable way.

Trends And Opportunities In Print/Document Fulfillment

By Curt Barry

Introduction

Like many industries, the printing and forms industry is undergoing a sea change in the area of print and document fulfillment. Digital printing, Print on Demand (POD), on-line electronic delivery of client communications and Portable Document Formats (PDF), web-based client servers, variable binding, and other technologies have created new opportunities for every one in the supply chain.

This chapter discusses:

- Trends Shaping Print and Document Fulfillment
- Collateral and Product Fulfillment Market
- Product Fulfillment Center Technologies
- Opportunities For Distributors and Printers
- Product Fulfillment Center Technologies
- The Letter Shop/Mail Shop of Tomorrow

Six Trends Shaping Print and Document Fulfillment

Trend #1: Companies Provide Both Electronic and Physical Fulfillment

Technology and the World Wide Web has created an entirely new playing field for meeting client print and document needs. The fully armed competitor of today and in the future will be able to provide both electronic fulfillment and warehousing (physical) fulfillment of document and printed materials.

A large portion of the printed materials distributed by industry, are now provided through electronic fulfillment. Electronic fulfillment has lowered the cost per unit, eliminated printed material obsolescence, created flexibility to tailor materials, improved turn around times, etc.

There is a right place for both electronic materials and fulfillment, and printed materials and physical document fulfillment. Is your company embracing and providing both to your clients?

Trend #2: Web Will Continue Innovation in Information

Here are three more things that the World Wide Web has brought to industry: easy access to information; speed of delivery; the customer is in control. During the 1990s, the dot.coms were going to destroy the printed paper catalog industry. That didn't happen. Today the average catalog often does 20% of its direct sales over the web and there is great synergy between the electronic "catalog" and the printed. The pure dot.coms have all but gone away. Even Amazon produces catalogs. Some of our business-to-business clients derive more than 50% of sales from the Web. The value of the World Wide Web is in the information it provides worldwide.

The electronic revolution was heralded to bring us into the paperless information age. That hasn't happened either. We still print off reams and reams of paper, distribute it to our coworkers and clients. The Web has given us on-line World Wide access to information. But we still rely on printed materials sometimes in a different form. The next generation of print fulfillment companies will harness technology even more.

Trend #3: Ability to Handle Product Fulfillment

As part of a total marketing program, large companies have over the years used "product" in their marketing efforts. There are a wide range of ways that companies use product. It may be emblematic product or it may offer a lifestyle product offering exclusive to their brand. Companies that have lead their clients in this transformation have often provided printed materials, collateral, promotional product and fulfillment to serve the total marketing needs. Many companies are moving into product fulfillment as the collateral fulfillment space becomes more competitive.

Trend #4: Value Added Services

Many aspects of service industries have become "commodities" and when that happens price becomes a key factor. It's no longer enough to provide printed materials. We have to combine it with other marketing services and add value.

Take for example lead generation. You may print and fulfill collateral for your client. But can you add call center services which better qualify the leads? Tie dealers, factories and headquarters together into the lead generation system? Host a web site or integrate the site back into the lead fulfillment system?

On the Internet (www.maritzrewards.com/rewards-toyota.html) there is an excellent Case Study of one such lead generation system that Maritz Rewards created for Toyota and Lexus marketing campaigns. According to Maritz Rewards' web site: "The results, Average fulfillment turnaround of 24 hours. Average fulfillment of 1,650 letters per day - 7,000 on peak days. Average of 300 Hot Leads per day and 700 Leads sent to Lead Delivery daily."

While I'm sure there was a large scale investment to set up the Toyota and Lexus lead management system. Clearly, the marketing challenges cited in the Case Study make it clear that printing and mailing collateral was no longer good enough for the client.

In our experience, when we add marketing value to the client's work we create longer term, profitable relationships which are much harder for competitors to take away.

The Maritz example also drives home that print and document fulfillment is in a broader sense a piece of the total marketing. Integration of marketing media – it isn't all print or direct mail. It's a combination of ways to reach the clients involving Web, print, direct mail, e-mail marketing, in-bound and outbound calls and other media where applicable.

Trend #5: Use of Third Party Fulfillment (3PF) Gains Acceptance

Outsourcing has become an accepted business model because companies have grown to recognize that fulfillment and logistics is not their core competency. Third party fulfillment (3 PF) often provides a lower cost per order or per piece distributed and faster turn around than what can be achieved internally by companies for which fulfillment is not a core competency. Additionally, the 3 PF client does not have to invest capital in the required technology, facilities and organization. 3 PF also allows clients to expand customer service, accommodate peak periods and call center over flow and gain high capacity.

Trend #6: Benchmarking, Best Practice and Certification

Few print shops bother to benchmark their costs and service levels. An axiom from the field of industrial engineering has it that you cannot improve what you haven't measured. Best example, is order turnaround. A decade ago, order turn around of up to 10 was acceptable to a collateral client. But today's systems and processes - as the Maritz Rewards' Case Study showed - must be geared toward 24-hour order turnaround times.

Another aspect to benchmarking should lead you to understand the cost of all transactions and services. It may lead you to examine whether you getting a fair price for your efforts. Or are you giving away services for free, when you could be charging for them. These free services may include "pay as you go" programs, becoming a "partner" in purchasing incentive products, not charging for account management fees, etc. Your competitor made be charging for these services. Every dollar saved goes right to your bottom line.

There are two general types of benchmarking - internal and external benchmarks. Internal benchmarking creates standards for key metrics and then reports these back to management. The most important benchmarks are those that you report internally and see improvement from season to season and year to year. External benchmarking takes place on a cooperative basis usually within an association, trade group or among similar companies in different parts of the country to protect confidentiality. Benchmarking combined with best practice implementation can increase your service levels, lower your costs, and boost your turnaround times.

Another key element learned from benchmarking is that in many business processes, 50% of cost is direct labor. Benchmarking should help us learn how to manage and control our largest component of cost.

In the last few years, we are seeing companies looking to use various certification programs to both differentiate themselves from the competition and raise their customer service levels. In general to achieve certification, you need to implement internal procedures and processes which raise your company's performance to a higher standard. In 3PF, we have seen companies such as Moulton Logistics Management (www.moultonlogistics.com), Budco (www.budco.com), and CPI Business Groups (www.cpigroups.com) become ISO certified (International Standards Organization). Or in Call Centers operations COPC certified (Customer Operations Performance standards). Depending on the industry that you serve – such as manufacturing - ISO standardization may be more common place.

Collateral and Product Fulfillment Market

Marketing data about the size of the collateral and product fulfillment is very limited. Third party fulfillment companies (3 PF) are small, a highly fragmented industry and regional in nature. There are literally hundreds to thousands of companies that offer fulfillment of collateral materials and products. This means there's a tremendous opportunity to grab future market share by 3PF service providers as it is difficult for any one company to dominate the market.

In one private survey that was conducted in 2002 of approximately 600 providers of fulfillment and mailing service companies, 75% of the respondents had client billings of $2 million or less and most are regional companies. Thirty (30) firms had sales between $20 and $50 million and 15 had sales over $50 million. Only 6% of these companies are involved in product fulfillment.

As we look at 3PF of product, we believe company sizes will also hold true – the majority will be companies with sales under $5 million annually.

What this says to us is that 3 PFs providing collateral fulfillment have the ability to compete in this marketplace from a size perspective. Secondly, product fulfillment is clearly where you should also look to the future to round out your clients' marketing offering.

Opportunities For Distributors and Printers

Your watchword should be carpe diem - "seize the day". With change of this magnitude, new opportunities always present themselves. The technology and benefits to the customer will not go away. Find the right ways to harness it to provide new services to your clients.

Distributors have long survived because they took a consultative approach to solving client problems. Clients still want to deal with companies and individuals that bring them solutions. These new technologies and electronic fulfillment are ripe with solutions awaiting client problems.

As we discussed in benchmarking, use its principles to fully understand your cost, service levels and processes and how to improve them.

If you're not in collateral and product fulfillment, spend priority time to explore what it will take for your organization to provide these services to your prospect and client base.

Then, there's customer service. One advantage to being small is that you can afford to give your clients the feeling that they are the "big fish in the small pond". While all the technology may sounds impressive, the reality is that many larger fulfillment companies have failed to stay technologically up to date. If you can't make the total capital investment, bring together alliances of service companies.

Product Fulfillment Center Technologies

There are several technologies which are essential to growth as you transition into product fulfillment.

Direct to Customer Systems

If you are going to provide collateral and product fulfillment, then direct to customer systems will be required to provide call center, marketing, merchandising, inventory forecasting and shipping/ manifesting support. These systems are considerable different from information systems employed in print and letter shop operations.

One of the critical differences is that many types of product fulfillment require payment with an order from bank and charge cards and check with order.

Another difference is in the inventory control functions. Because product has a much higher dollar value and is often not a give away, the service provider must now have an accurate inventory management system to the SKU (color-size level). In the printing industry, a quantity tolerance of plus or minus 10% is acceptable. However, the costs are much higher in product fulfillment than paper costs. Customers expect—and contractually get—stated inventory overages and shrinkages that are less than 1%.

In more complex, larger warehouse environments, the inventory systems are integrated with Radio Frequency (RF) for scanning and tracking inventory from receiving, stock putaway, through picking, packing, shipping and manifesting. This dramatically improves the accuracy of client inventory by inventory location. RF scanning systems reduces labor involved in picking, managing inventory, stock cycle counting, shipping/manifesting. In turn, scanning the outbound package as it leaves the warehouse allows the shipping data to be updated back into the customer service system and to create the invoice data from the scanned transaction. This gives you the ability to track the client packages through expedited carrier systems and also to answer questions about when you shipped the order.

Customer Contact or Call Center Operations Technologies

Most collateral fulfillment companies do not offer call center consulting services. Forward thinking companies will jump on this trend because it allows users of collateral to do business with a single entity. Adding technology may cost you in the near term, but you'll reap the rewards of providing value-added services to your clients.

Inbound call programs

Progressive users of call centers are moving from looking at inbound representatives as order takers to being sales-oriented and making sales. Thanks to effective cross selling and upselling of services the average order increases significantly (typically 2% to 4%) without the corresponding cost increase.

Outbound call programs

While the Federal Trade Commission (FTC) guidelines for this have changed in 2003, companies can still make outbound calls with consumers and businesses that they have a prior relationship with. While this needs to be tastefully, professionally and legally done, this is still a major opportunity for increasing sales and generating leads for which you have an established relationship (lead inquiry or sale).

Servicing the Web customer

A significant portion of Web customers abort the transaction because of confusion about the site or they do not wish to enter a credit card number over the Web. An essential function of the call center is to service this rapidly growing segment of business. Other functions today's call centers provide are web chat and e-mail inquiry resolution to customer questions.

Interactive Voice Response (IVR) Capability

IVR capability is the cheapest way in terms of cost per transaction to service a customer for a simple transaction such as placing a simple order, inquiring on a back order, etc. There is still reluctance by management to fully utilize technology. But look at the self serve nature of the Web or bank ATMs. Who would have thought 10 years ago that a high percentage of transactions would be of customer self serve in nature.

Automatic Call Distributor (ACD)

Automatic Call Distributors (ACDs) are telephone switches used in call centers to manage call center operations, identify and respond to call volume and fluctuations in your business. Call center staffing software reads information from real-time or batch data will improve coverage and your agent's productivity. The ability to monitoring calls for quality assurance and have 24/7 capability are essential to your success.

The Letter Shop/Mail Shop of Tomorrow

No one has a crystal ball but here is what we see happening based on current market forces and company strategies. Most lettershops/mail shops compete on a regional basis. As the competition increases and price becomes more of an issue, we see lettershops slowly moving to expand their services. Electronic and physical fulfillment are such offerings.

As the clients needs grow, lettershops will move into product fulfillment of premiums and incentives to round out client marketing requirements.

Additionally, we see industry leaders in product fulfillment performing double duty in the collateral fulfillment. This puts lettershops into competition with thousands of other firms already in fulfillment of promotional products and consumer products offerings.

As the lettershop/mail shop changes its marketing to include fulfillment, the lettershops will compete on a national scale which, in turn, increases the capital requirements needed to build the infrastructure for warehousing, customer contact center, systems and organizational perspectives.

Most lettershops are already involved in the marketing and mailing strategies of its clients. As the requirements change from getting the lead to making the sale, your marketing efforts will segue to highly sophisticated database marketing technologies and customer contact center technologies.

1688635